Praise for *Reflec*

"Navy Phim brilliantly weaves a story of being Khmer and American like an intricate pattern of the *Sampot Hole* (Khmer Silk Skirt). Her narrative represents many Khmer-American voices of the post Khmer Rouge generation searching for identity. She writes with a candor and passion that expresses a faithful soul."

—Sovathana Sokhom, former consultant to the United Nations in Cambodia

"With a passion for speaking the truth, Navy delivers a well-written book that touches on the global issues of political correctness, skin color, class status and socio-economic background. Her narrative takes readers on a journey through her past and present and engages them on discussions of cultural diversity, spirituality, beauty and justice for all. I highly recommend this personal story of success and stigma faced by immigrants in America to educators of immigrant students."

—Alex Morales, University Instructor, Multicultural Education,

Reflections of a Khmer Soul

Fonty

XI/2021

Reflections of a Khmer Soul

NAVY PHIM

Reflections of a Khmer Soul

Published by Wheatmark™
610 East Delano Street, Suite 104
Tucson, Arizona 85705 U.S.A.
www.wheatmark.com

International Standard Book Number:
    978-1-58736-861-5
Library of Congress Control Number: 2007926800

Contents

CONTENTS   ix

Part Five: Musings of a Traveler

Part Six: Remembrance and Celebration

Part Seven: Final Thoughts

x CONTENTS

Foreword

This new work, by a Khmer American woman born in April 1975, just as her country was plunged into the horrors of the Khmer Rouge regime, is not another first person narrative of the events of that time. Rather, it is a narrative of a personal journey exploring the legacy of being ethnic Cambodian in the aftermath of Pol Pot, of living with the stories of war that live as a "disorderly chaos churning in my head." Ms. Phim is not the daughter of urban elites banished to the countryside as "new" people, as all of those to publish first person accounts have been to date. Her family members were farmers, and this lends a different tone to her perspective. Her own early memories are from life in refugee camps in Thailand where Thai soldiers are the ogres of myth, and growing up in the United States being the responsible older daughter. Some of her themes will resonate across the lives of other Asian American daughters, for example: white skin and pointed noses – what conceptions of beauty to embrace, living with a name that Euro-Americans have trouble pronouncing, finding healing in "coining", and living with responsibility to family. But other topics are clearly and pointedly only for Khmer, the draw to return to the motherland despite and because of the heartache there; a pride in things Khmer – from Angkor Wat to beautiful silks to soothing Khmer melodies; an appreciation and acceptance of Khmer standards of female modesty; and most difficult of all – coming to terms with the violence of Khmer Rouge period. Who was to blame? The "ignorant" peasants, tricked by the Western educated Marxists, or the corrupt and exploitative urban elite who treated those beneath them with great cruelty? The discussion Ms. Phim weaves has important ramifications for life in contemporary Cambodia. In the second half of the manuscript Ms. Phim does not stay home as a dutiful daughter, but travels to many countries from Thailand to Peru, writing that growing up as a refugee set her on the course of a nomad. The book is an interesting contribution to the literature on Asian Americans, Cambodian Americans and growing up as a transnational. It will likely be most powerful when read by other Khmer Americans who wrestle with the same demons and live with the same legacy.

—Dr. Judy Ledgerwood, Associate Professor and Department Chair, Cultural Anthropology, Northern Illinois University, March 2007

PART ONE

Reveries and Memories

Letter to the World

Dear World, I cannot fight and die for you, but I can speak a little on your behalf, examining the sentiments of war and the wasted blood that has spilled over you. I am an earth child rooted in Cambodia. I have lived a life that requests expression and understanding.

Words, thoughts, scenarios, and sentence structures float in my head attempting to materialize. I must capture them before they dissolve into fleeting thoughts. I write because I have something to say. I write to give voice to love and passion, anger and hope, my mothers, my country, and the world. I write about memories and souls.

California: April 2005

In 2005, on April 9, I turned thirty. April 17 of that year marked the thirtieth anniversary of the Year Zero. It was an invention of the Khmer Rouge's communistic utopia that caused nearly two million deaths, untold suffering, and lingering trauma.

When I turned thirty, it was just another day. I was sitting in a coffee shop when a friend came by and offered to take me flying as a birthday gift. Likewise, April 17 had always been just another day, but in April 2005, the terrifying vestiges of the Killing Fields brought conflict and division to the Cambodian community of Long Beach, California. The few weeks leading to April 17 were charged with heated discussions and arguments between friends and strangers and within families. As April drifted away, I resumed my writing. I had worked on this collection of memories since the summer of 2004, but most of the stories had been written, rewritten, and remembered many times in an attempt to express my experiences in the refugee camps and comprehend the atrocities of the Killing Fields.

Cambodia: April 1975

The sounds of bombs and gunshots welcomed me into the world. Panic-stricken screams, footsteps pounding the ground, people running desperately for shelter, and the alarming cries of separated families charged the air in Cambodia on April 9, 1975.

My mother was nine months pregnant. She peddled an old bicycle to flee her farmland, which had become a battlefield. I was safe and comforted in her womb, but not for long. Later that night, she went into labor and I was born. During her bicycle escape, she was separated from my father, but they found each other and reunited as a family with me as their newborn, first child.

Sing me a song to erase the sounds of war that echo in my memories. Write me a melody to soothe my baby soul. Hum me a silent tune of love.

Hush my little darling
Let me hold you and cuddle you
Gently and softly against my chest
Let my heartbeat be a muse
To inspire your new life on earth
Let my heartbeat be a guiding light
To lead you through this journey
Hush my little darling
Listen to my heartbeat
To feel the vibration of love

Reverie

I am a child of a war-ravaged country. The preceding sentence, and even the phrase *war-ravaged country,* or the word alone, *war-ravaged,* can fuel the imagination of readers and listeners with gory pictures of death, butchered bodies, bloody streets, rolling tanks, bombed cities, burning fires, smoke-darkened skies, and scattered people scrambling and crying, trying to make sense of their experiences. But when you see the sentence *I am a survivor of the Killing Fields,* your imagination awakens to the human spirit and its ability to survive. Surviving a war-ravaged country makes one seem heroic. As I write *I am a child of a war-ravaged country* and then *I am a survivor of the Killing Fields,* I almost believe in my own heroism. But what do I remember from being a *war-ravaged* child? Bits and pieces of a million stories that I have to make sense of; words and sounds that I need to transcribe into a story.

To think of myself as a survivor of the Killing Fields is strange. I did not live through the Killing Fields, *per se,* but I am trying to understand the pain, loss, dehumanization, and post-traumatic syndrome that lingered in the minds of many survivors. I was merely an infant. I was born in April 1975, the month and year the Khmer Rouge took over. This is a more interesting story, and in listening to my mother, the day I was born made me special in a strange way. Maybe it was only meant to serve as a reminder for me, and if I believed that I was special, what would I do to live up to it? She said that I was born the day the Khmer Rouge took over and that I was a true child of "A-Pot." My mother knows the day, the month, and the feature of the moon when I was born, but she is unable to translate it into the Western calendar and give me an exact date. The infamous day that the Khmer Rouge took Phnom Penh was April 17, 1975, but I was probably born a week or more prior to that day because the Khmer Rouge gained victory over the provinces before Phnom Penh. Many non-Khmers and a few Khmers could not grasp how my own mother did not know the date of my birth. They seem appalled by it, but I could not understand why they are dismayed because how many of their parents know the feature of the moon on their birthday and how long ago since the moon was full. My mother knows that I was born on the 13th day of the waning moon in April of 1975 and I still stake claim to my birthday and the way my mother remembers it as something special.

Was I a true child of "A-Pot"? A-Pot is a word that describes the Pol Pot regime with much vehemence if we said it to be so. I was born into it and lived through it from 1975 to 1979. It is nothing to be proud of and nothing to be ashamed of. As a believer of what was written in the stars, I was meant to be born on that day, at that time, in that country, with that soul. A Khmer soul. A soul that has questions, a soul that needs to vindicate the actions of her countrymen and fellow human beings.

Explanation

It is nothing to be proud of and nothing to be ashamed of. I was wary of this sentence because it may sound like I do not feel shame for what took place in 1975 to 1979. In a way, that is exactly what I am saying. I should not feel shame for being born into Cambodia and for being Khmer. I was not responsible for the Killing Fields and did not participate in the killings. This conclusion came out of shame.

On my travels, I have met people who unwittingly said to me, "You are from Cambodia, you're Khmer Rouge." Insensitivity and possibly ignorance produce this comment. I am speechless. I am too shocked to defend myself, too shocked to explain that I am not a Khmer Rouge and I do not appreciate being associated with them. Others have said, "Your country and people are crazy." I cringe at the statement. I feel ashamed then, ashamed of my country and my people.

In Nepal, I met a man who spoke perfect English. He attended college in America in the 1970s and protested against the Vietnam War. He was knowledgeable about the history of Cambodia and offered words of sympathy. I felt open to share and discuss my knowledge of Cambodia with him. Our conversations were the catalyst for the realization that I should not carry the shame on my own. As an individual being, separate from my country, I carry no shame. But being Cambodian requires a lot of *explanation*. For instance, Wednesday, April 9, 1975, was the day of my birth and the day the Khmer Rouge took over the Province of Battambang. However, Phnom Penh did not fall until Thursday, April 17, 1975.

For years, when I tried to figure out my birthday on the Western calendar, I was perplexed because the day the Khmer Rouge took over did not match my birthday.

I studied the Khmer calendar and discovered that the thirteenth day of the waning moon meant that it was two days before the new moon. In April 1975, two days before the new moon was Wednesday, April 9. I was born on a Wednesday, the thirteenth day of the waning moon when the Khmer Rouge took over Battambang.

My driver's license has a birthday that my parents devised for the paperwork to come to America. They chose consecutive months—April, May, June, and July— for the birthday of each family member and, of course, being the third person in the family (after my mother and father), I was given a June birthday, making me two months younger than I really am. But living in America, a culture that gives greater value to youth, it is fine by me to be two months younger. I call June "my legal birthday" and what is legal for many Cambodians may not be real or correct.

Churning Memories

The stories of the war are a disorderly chaos churning in my head. I do not remember the war or life under the Khmer Rouge regime, but I possess the memories of my parents, relatives, and friends. These are their memories, but they have been incorporated into my own. These stories are told with sadness in their eyes, voices, and remembrances. Some are told with humor and pride; other stories show human compassion.

Fear and uncertainty were a part of my parents' lives even prior to 1975, especially because my mother lived in an isolated village. There were wayward and disillusioned soldiers roaming around, and one of them approached her as she was lugging water to her home. By chance, her friend was visiting at the time, and the soldier was deterred. But if there were no war, there would be no wayward soldiers roaming around causing concerns for her chastity and safety.

My churning memories of the war also include an anecdote regarding my birth and Khmer superstition. Cambodians believed that a birthmark is a scar from a previous life, a remnant of a trauma so great it remains with us. They also believe that when you dream about a dead person asking to live with you, it means that the child you are carrying is the reincarnation of that person. My mother had a fifteen-year-old niece who died in 1972 or 1973 from a stray bullet to her stomach (from the American bombing?). Before I was born, my mother dreamt of her deceased niece asking for shelter. She wanted to live with my mother because her own mother had too many children to feed. When I was born, I had a birthmark on my stomach in the same location of her death wound. According to the story of my birth, I am an incarnation of the war victim, a Khmer belief for my Khmer soul.

Another story that my mother delightfully repeats is the story of my birth. People were scattered everywhere, trying to stay out of the line of fire. My mother and father were separated. My pregnant mother peddled her bicycle to escape the shells and arrived in Lavey, a village near *Phnom Krapeh*, the Crocodile Mountain. Later that night, my mother went into labor and I was born with a soft, swollen head that she attributed to the bicycle ride.

I was small and frail, struggling to inhale air into my lungs and breathe life into my soul. I survived, but few believed that I would; the expressions on my aunts' and uncles' faces mirrored that uncertainty. Three months later, I was healthy and strong. My relatives confessed their true feelings and my mother was offended. For her, this is a story of triumph and survival against great obstacles, hers and mine—one of these churning memories of war stories.

The Road to America

I had sporadically heard stories about the war and life in Cambodia, but I had never asked my parents specific questions about their life under the Khmer Rouge. After twenty years in the United States and having acquired some historical knowledge through books and other sources, I asked my mother what her life was like under the Khmer Rouge and her reasons for leaving Cambodia. I wanted to hear her rationale, but hers was not the answer that I had anticipated.

The cruelty of the regime was different in each region.

The Khmer Rouge's murderous vendetta was largely directed toward families of soldiers who served under Lon Nol and city dwellers whose livelihood did not depend on farming; but eventually, they turned on anyone who might be against them. This could be their own members or someone hiding food or being too sick to work.

During the war, soldiers from both sides stumbled into my mother's village and a well-respected elder in the village offered assistance to all. He made cryptic remarks about taking the American's side but as a religious person, his kindness was extended to everybody. When the Khmer Rouge took over, they put him and the commune leaders in charge of the village. There were no outsiders and no Khmer Rouge controlling my mother's village. The existing leadership became the new Khmer Rouge leaders.

The village was set up like the rest of the country: people worked and ate communally and the townspeople of Battambang were sent to villages. But unlike other parts of the country, they were allowed to tend to the garden around their huts and keep whatever they were able to grow. My mother was proud that the villagers and the townspeople coexisted peacefully and possible crises were resolved before they escalated. A woman from the town of Battambang boasted about her life of luxury prior to the Khmer Rouge regime, but the wise elder advised her to curb her tongue. She heeded the warning and the village continued to prosper and exist in harmony, defying the Khmer Rouge regime's trademarks of fear and bickering.

Two years into the regime, the village leadership was replaced. My mother's recollection of this coincides with the different concurrent autobiographies I have read. There seemed to be a two-year marker where the Khmer Rouge restructured their policy and replaced their leadership in villages across the country because the old leaders were too lenient and the labor system was not producing results. The Khmer Rouge soldiers who arrived for the restructuring killed the people they had once placed in charged. One of the original leaders survived the massacre. I remember my mother telling me when I was younger that he was a former Khmer Rouge. I wondered why she was speaking to him, but I finally understood that he was among the kind and lenient "Khmer Rouge." His wife was not as fortunate; she was among those that were brutally slaughtered. When my mother talks about her death, there is an incomprehensible look on her face as her mind flashes to a distant memory and an event that she will never be able to explain.

Under the new leadership, life was harder but still better in my parents' village than in most of the country. Mother had to hide food and secretly feed me at night. One day as she was feeding me, I loudly exclaimed, "Jackfruit! More jackfruit!" As I demanded to be fed, several Khmer Rouge soldiers were strolling behind our hut. At that moment, my parents thought they would be killed for hiding food, a betrayal that had caused many people to be murdered under the regime. Fortunately, the Khmer Rouge were speaking too loudly to hear me.

My parents did not have family members who were tortured and slaughtered once the Khmer Rouge was in power. However, they had relatives who were forced into marriages arranged by *Angka*, the term used to describe the Khmer Rouge organization. I have heard stories of their marriages and how they were separated after the wedding for months before consummating it. I heard of their courtships during this strange time and their decisions to stay together.

Incorporated within these stories was a story about my parents' loyal dog. During the last year of the regime, the dog was getting thinner and thinner, and one day it disappeared. My mother searched for it but it was futile, and she knew then that someone had killed it. She cursed the person who had killed it, but another part of her understood and accepted that someone had killed it because they were starving. My mother always made it clear that Khmer people do not eat dogs. They keep them as pets to safeguard the family and their property. People only ate them during the war when they were dying of hunger (at least people from her part of Cambodia).

My mother confessed that she had eaten dog meat during the Khmer Rouge regime. When she was pregnant with my brother, she had a craving for meat. One day, my father came home with a piece of cooked meat. He gave it to her and she offered to split it with him, but he refused her offer. My mother was suspicious that it might have been dog meat but her craving was strong. She ate it. It was years later before she finally asked my father what kind of meat it was and he confirmed that it was dog meat.

The story of their life under the Khmer Rouge regime surprised me. I knew that as farmers, they did not face the risk of being killed, but I did not know that life was moderately comfortable compared to the rest of the country. I asked her in surprise, "Why did you leave Cambodia?"

My mother portrayed the road to America as packed with accidental good fortune and a dash of good karma. Following the liberation/invasion by the Vietnamese, the Khmer Rouge scattered into hiding. My parents returned to their life as farmers surviving with the crops and riches they possessed, but my paternal grandparents were not as lucky. They requested my parents to accompany them to Thailand to *rot-pon*. *Rot-pon* was the term for the smuggling of goods from Thailand to sell in Cambodia for profit—it was a way of making a living—smuggling and dealing with the black market. This was the reason my parents left Cambodia—for the purpose of *rot-pon* and *rok-see*, which means to make a living.

My parents had relatives who had left for Thailand months earlier and other relatives who had joined them later. There were also relatives who refused to go because they had heard of the danger involved and did not want to risk the lives of their family members. Those individuals who remained have regretted their decision and they insisted on telling me so when I finally met them during my visits to Cambodia. My parents packed all of their belongings into their cow-drawn cart and journeyed to an unknown destiny after saying their good-byes to family and friends who chose to remain in Cambodia.

The road to Thailand was full of hazards, but my mother also recalled stories of good fortune. The journey depleted all of their resources. When they finally arrived in Thailand in the city of Nong-Chan, they had to sell their cow and cart. At that point, there was no turning back.

In Nong-Chan, they were reunited with relatives who had left Cambodia earlier. They rejoiced at the reunion, but felt unsure of the future. Thai helicopters were flying over them, telling the confused Cambodian refugees to leave Thailand. As they tried to figure out where to go, my parents saw a huge crowd traveling together in a direction. My parents asked where they were heading, and people in the crowd told them about refugee camps being set up. My parents and other relatives followed the group and were transported by bus to Kao-I-Dang. From there, they awaited their transfer into what people in the refugee camps termed the "third country," which would be any one of the many countries that sponsored Cambodian refugees. After four years in different camps, my family was sponsored to America.

Refugee Markets

Once upon a time, not long ago yet at times it feels like a lifetime ago, I was a young peddler. It was my first occupation and I was fairly good at it, but it was not my occupation of choice. It was forced upon me by my mother. At six years old, I worked as a vendor to supplement our livelihood as we resided in various refugee camps. My mother, being an enterprising and determined woman, decided to participate in the markets that were set up in the camps, the legal markets as well as the illegal ones. In Sakeo, the market was operated legally and my mother and I sold French bread at a stall in the market. Early in the morning, I walked to our stall and managed it alone while my mother was out in the neighborhoods selling bread at people's houses. Once she had navigated all of her usual routes, she came to the stall to relieve me of my duty.

In Khao-I-Dang, the market was operated illegally, but it was bustling and profitable. My duty in Khao-I-Dang included touting the products around the neighborhoods and selling them at the market. While my mother was at the market, I walked around the neighborhoods selling *nom-kroch,* shouting *"Nom-kroch! Nom-kroch!"* Besides *nom-kroch,* I also sold different products like salt, pepper, and MSG.

When I returned to Cambodia and saw young merchants touting their products, I remembered my life as a peddler in the refugee camps and how much I hated walking around with my merchandise feeling afraid of meeting Thai soldiers. Sometimes, I walked around silently, not shouting out the name of my products to avoid Thai soldiers.

Sometimes, my mother sent me to the market to sell the products. Thai soldiers would sporadically raid the market, catching as many people as they could and confiscating their merchandise. A few hours after the raid, the market would be bustling with vendors and buyers again, bargaining and buying what they needed.

Once or twice, people that we knew ran into our hut, asking for refuge from the soldiers that were confiscating their livelihood. Once or twice, my mother and I had also run into the huts of people that we knew, asking for refuge. We helped each other, cheating the system, keeping the market alive.

Being a peddler was not my chosen occupation. I preferred playing with my friends, but in the refugee camps, I was a peddler. I also played, explored, and acted like a child, creating fond memories.

Thai Ogres

American children are afraid of monsters living under their beds and in their closets. I grew up with stories of *preai* and *ab*, menacing creatures that inhabit Cambodian legends of horror. I was frightened of *preai* and *ab*, but there were even scarier monsters in the refugee camps.

The scary ogres in the refugee camps were Thai soldiers. I had heard stories of their cruelty and was chased by them when I worked at the illegal market in the refugee camps. I had also seen them parading and beating men who were caught smuggling. The Thai soldiers were more frightening than *preai* or *ab*. I avoided making eye contact with them, glancing away when their gaze turned in my direction.

One fateful day, as I was walking home from the market, I had an encounter with a Thai soldier. My mother had sent me home with food from the market. I was a dutiful child walking cautiously on the side of the road to avoid traffic. Unfortunately, there were two careless children chasing each other in the middle of the road, probably playing hide-and-seek. It happened that a Thai soldier on a bicycle was riding on that very same road. In an attempt to avoid hitting them, he swerved to the side and knocked me down. He toppled off his bike and landed in the ditch near the road.

I fell down, skinning my knees and elbows. My food tumbled in different directions. After I stood up and oriented myself, I saw the Thai soldier with his bike on top of him in the ditch. As soon as I realized what I had done, I ran, leaving my shoes and food behind. It had never occurred to me that I was the one that had been wronged.

I arrived home, delirious, disheveled, and frightened. My grandparents, aunts, and uncles tried to get me to talk, but I was in shock. I do not remember much of what happened after that or how they got the story out of me. But they still talk about the incident. In my madness, I went into the house and came out disguised in rags, covering my head with an old, dirty *sampot*, talking, shaking, and crying all at once.

I have blocked out many parts of the incident, but I remember returning for the food and shoes with my mother. Someone went to the market to find my mother and bring her to the house. I remembered being reluctant, frightened, and unconvinced when my mother told me it was not my fault. When we arrived, there were still spectators standing around, trying to understand what had happened. My mother told the crowd that I was the child involved with the accident. She asked them if they saw the food that I was carrying. Someone brought out the food and the shoes I had left behind.

People were eager to express their sympathy and discuss the incident. My mother explained that I had run away, afraid of being punished. They told my mother that the Thai soldier was extremely concerned and had asked to see the child that he had accidentally knocked down. But no one could find me. He had already left by the time we got there. Even though they told us that he was concerned about me, I was grateful that he was gone.

I rarely think about the incident and many other incidents that took place in the refugee camps, but from time to time, I remember. I remember different incidents on different days when my friends and I talk about our lives. I remember different incidents when I read stories that trigger those memories.

In 1998, I participated in a study abroad program in Thailand. For the first month, I lived with a host family. Every morning, I peddled an old bicycle to Chiang Mai University, passing by a Thai military base. I remembered the incident with the Thai soldier. I laughed at myself then, at the fear that I had. I laughed at the "madness" that I felt that day. I laughed because I am my family's amusing story. I came face to face with my childhood ogre and came to terms with that particular childhood fear, the monster under my bed, the scariest ogre of all, Thai soldiers.

Hunger and Hospitality

When an outsider talks about a group of people they came into contact with, it is their hospitality that determines if the people are welcoming and cordial. Cambodian hospitality is a thing to be praised. Hospitality is almost always in the form of food, feeding the guests, making sure they are comfortable and enjoying their stay. When we first came to America, soda was an important part of the hospitality food for guests, whether they were strangers, family friends, or relatives. It was a special type of refreshment, different and exciting, representing America and everything that we had been dreaming about in the camps.

These soft drinks fizzled as we poured them into a glass of ice for our guests, signifying our new life and newfound wealth, an abundance of food that can be shared without restraint.

My mother is great at making friends with the neighbors. She taught me a hospitality that shows the generosity of village life with a mixture of the Buddhist concept of charity. My mother loves to share the food she cooks with our neighbors. Once she finishes cooking, she scoops the food into a bowl and tells me to take it over to the neighbors. She explains that when you are giving something to anyone, make sure that you are giving it with your heart, which means giving them the first bowl, instead of the leftover that you no longer want. She said if we were giving away unsavory crumbs, the dishonest intention hidden in this charitable act would bring forth bad karma.

I love my mother and her generous traits, but I remember a time when generosity was not affordable. One of my friends in Khao-I-Dang came over to visit and it was close to lunchtime. My friend may have chosen to stay because she was not getting enough food to eat at home because she had many more siblings than I did. She may have also chosen to stay in order to have two meals, but in either case, my mother was hesitant to invite her to eat with us. My mother diplomatically mentioned that it was lunchtime and suggested that my friend go home, which was actually quite rude. But my friend answered that she would rather stay and visit as long as possible. My mother then told her that she could eat with us, but we only had rice and salt. My friend happily exclaimed that rice was great with salt. The three of us ate together, rice and salt, and there may have been some fish to go with our rice, but it was the best food I tasted. I was eating my meal with my mother and my friend. Even at that age, I knew that

it was a sacrifice for my mother to allow my friend to eat
with us.

Honoring Their Laughter

The survivors of the Killing Fields—my parents, relatives, and their friends—still reminisce about the war and
Cambodia. The pain and suffering from the war are still a
part of their conversation; some incidents are remembered
with sadness in their eyes and others are remembered with
laughter. They also feel nostalgia for their former life as
farmers and the days of peace before the war.

But life goes on…. And it goes on in an altogether
different setting and environment, *a different country to be
exact.* My parents did not need to teach me how to farm
or tend the land. I needed to learn how to drive, get my
driver's license, and be independent. During my last year
in high school, my father finally took the time to give me
driving lessons. I was a slow learner and a fidgety and
nervous driver. I knew that I frightened him a few times
on the outing, but he never showed it. He was always calm.
He never yelled or lost his temper when he was in the car
with me, no matter what scary maneuvers I was attempting.

I never knew what kind of fears the driving lessons
stirred in him. But during a family reunion, my father re-
layed my driving lessons to the relatives. He was the cen-
ter of attention and the narrator of a hilarious story. He
began soberly by telling them that I was a difficult student,
slow to grasp the concepts of driving and the rules of the
road. But his voice boomed when he said that every time
he went on the road with me, he thought this was it, he
might not make it back to see the face of his beloved wife

and children again. Everyone roared with laughter, especially when he concluded by saying that it was scarier than
living under the Khmer Rouge and the chance of death
during the driving lessons was greater. And I thought to
myself that the people who are laughing and joking had
lived through the Khmer Rouge, but they can compare an
experience to it and see humor. They were expressing a
fundamentally important characteristic of the human spirit: the ability to survive and heal.

Their laughter also functioned as a reminder that in
order to honor their experiences and survival of the Killing Fields, I should learn as much as possible about the
Khmer Rouge regime and what happened to people living
under it, the death, the torture, the horror, and the inhu-
manity. I need to educate myself and put these thoughts
into words to understand my own feelings on the matter.

The Dream Child

My younger brother, Phavoeung, was born in 1978,
three years after me and one year before the Khmer Rouge
regime came to an end. My mother told me that I was
teased and taunted mercilessly on the day of his birth.
They told me that with a new baby in the family, my parents would not have time to secretly feed me at night or
love me anymore. It was a cruel joke.

We were the only two kids in the family before coming
to America because my mother, like many other women
living in the camps, participated in a birth control program. In America, without the restriction of a birth control program, my three younger siblings were born, a
sister and twin brothers, the youngest of the family.

My brother's name is Phavoeung—I am not even going to disclose how to pronounce it properly, but it has

two syllables. *Ah-Vouch* is a nickname I gave him. It means *monkey* or the archetypal name for a *pet monkey*. He is my little brother, my little monkey boy. The most interesting mispronunciation of his name is Fa-Ve-Ong, sounding almost like Fabio, the sexy symbol on the cover of old romance books.

For many Cambodians, an indication that a woman is pregnant takes place in her dream where she is given jewelry, usually a ring or necklace. Jewelry is something precious and valuable; thus, a child is seen and received as wealth in the family. Many Cambodians also believe that when one is meant to receive a certain fortune (some type of good luck) but a baby is born to the family, the luck has been converted to the fortune of having a child. Whether or not this is the preferred method of fortune is up to each family and what was needed at the time, another child or money to feed the children they already have?

For my mother, a sign of her pregnancy with my brother also came in the form of a dream like the one that foretold her pregnancy with me. She met a woman in her dream who gave her a shirt. The woman explained that the shirt came from a foreign country, asserting its value and importance. Upon waking up, my mother had an inkling that she was with child. She also felt that the dream foretold that she was carrying a special child. Throughout his life, she observed him to see how different and special he would be.

Well, little brother, tell me, what will you do to live up to our mother's idea of you being a special human being?

The Older Sister

My parents, like many Cambodian mothers and fathers, wanted their first-born to be a girl. The older sister would care for the younger children and cook for the family; thus, I am a wanted child, the oldest girl. For most of my life, I felt more like a mother than a sister.

Most Cambodian parents like to give their children names that bear similarity to each other to tie them together as siblings. I was not able to see the connection in our names, but my mother told me the v-sound linked us together: Navy, Phavoeung and Savuth. James and John are different from the three of us, but are linked to each other in their own special way by the J-sound and by being twins. They were the two children that were given American names.

At my house, no one called my sister Savuth. When she was a toddler, wobbling around the house, my grandmother saw the similarity between her way of walking and a character in a Thai movie named Mai and called her Mai. Later on, she became Mikey. Every family member calls her Mai or Mikey but she goes by Savuth at school. She seems proud of her given Khmer name, and uses it every chance she gets even though none of her friends can say it correctly.

Mikey was a compulsive baby. When she was overly hyperactive, I would place a piece of tape on her hand and she would stop in her tracks and spend hours pulling at the tape. I was thirteen years old and I felt proud of myself for coming up with this technique to curb her wired behavior. I had another bright idea to keep my three youngest siblings in line: I would put my three American-born siblings on a bed and play a pretend game with them. The bed was a boat and it was surrounded with crocodiles. The game worked because they were afraid to leave the boat, afraid of running into the invisible crocodiles. When they were in high school, I explained the reason behind this game, but they did not find it amusing. They told me, "*Bong Vy*, that is called child abuse." I am *Bong Vy*, older sister Vy. Vy, the short version of my name, is used by my family. Child abuse! I think not. I had to outsmart those brats because there were three of them and only one of me.

I was the perfect daughter, helping out around the house, cooking and taking care of my younger siblings as my parents slaved away at their sewing machines. I started high school when we moved to Long Beach, a city riddled with Cambodian gangsters, gang wars, drive-by shootings, and teenage pregnancies.

Dealing with a willful and unruly teenage daughter came later for my parents, when my sister started high school. I was a goody two-shoes, except for the talking back part. I did not always listen and do what they wanted me to do at home, but otherwise, I was doing well in school and was not involved in anything that would embarrass them: drugs, gangs, or sex.

But I have not been the perfect daughter for some time now because of my willful independence.

Refugee Communities

In the refugee camps in Thailand, I only remember other Cambodian people, but the Philippines was a transitional location, preparing all types of refugees for our sponsored country. My family was sent to the Philippines in 1983 when I was eight years old after living and moving between various refugee camps in Thailand for four years. In the Philippines, everyone was happier because we had been selected for the "third country."

Life was more relaxed with different leisure activities. We swam in a gushing creek and took day trips to the mountain. I went to the beach for the first time with the Cambodian community in a taxi or a bus. Many of us still have pictures of ourselves at the beach and the creek; rem-

iniscent of sweet memories. We attended English classes
to prepare for our new country. I vaguely remember my
English teacher who took us to her house to watch *Snow
White.*

Life in the Philippines was also different because it included different refugee communities. The Khmer, Vietnamese, and Laos refugees were living in close proximity
to each other, but separately, waiting for their departures.
They were people that had similar experiences; Vietnamese and Laos were also escaping from communism and
wars in their country.

I did not know about their experiences then or much
of anything about the history of our countries, but I was
aware of the animosity and the distrust of our historical
enemy—the Vietnamese. The refugee communities in the
Philippines represented the configuration of Southeast
Asia with Cambodia, Laos, and Vietnam, neighboring
countries, living as neighbors, but we stayed with our own
kind. I walked to school and played with my own people.
We did not make friends with the others. But most dis-
turbingly, we used to have cursing matches, the group of
Vietnamese and Khmer cursing at each other, the Khmer
cursing in Vietnamese and the Vietnamese cursing in
Khmer. The Vietnamese and Laos also cursed at each other as did the Laos and the Khmer.

Looking back now, I see the conflict between us, but
a year later, when I was in America, life shifted 180-de-
grees. The Vietnamese, Laos, Thais, and Khmers were all
friends and classmates, living in America, adjusting to our
new home and bonding together as the people of Southeast Asia.

Memories

Distant memories of the refugee camps refuse to be buried and forgotten. These memories demand a celebration of their existence. I remember…going to school, saving up for sweets, and watching cartoons in classes on special occasions. I remember that my best customer in the refugee camp was the wife of a notorious thief. Everyday, she bought *nom-kroch* from me using the money that her husband obtained from robbing refugees.

I remember going to the interview in Thailand… the interview that would bring us closer to the "third country" and security. I remember meeting a Thai boy that was hunting grasshoppers. He slashed his stick on the ground against the hundreds of grasshoppers, killing and decapitating many at once. He picked one up, broke off the head and gave it to me. He said, "Eat it." I understand the Thai word for eat, but that was the extent of our conversation. I followed him around for a bit before going back to my parents.

I was a curious child, with many accidents to my name. There was the encounter with the Thai soldier on a bike, but it was not my fault. I have stitches on my forehead and my ear. My forehead—I was testing out my ability to hop up the stair on one foot. I failed. In another incident, I ran to the market and slipped on spilt water, crashing against a stall, slitting a gash in my ear.

I remember… the bathroom door in the refugee camp did not close completely and my cousin asked me to lean against it while she was inside. When she was ready to leave, she told me to move, but I wanted to know what would happen if I did not move. The metal door cut the back of my leg leaving an ugly scar. I learn from trying, failure, success, and pain.

Memories of a distant life. Sometimes, I suppress

memories of that life of long ago. Sometimes, in an instant, I am transported to it, reliving the memories of my past because a simple song or scent revives it.

I feel older and wiser now, more passionate and angry, more loving and understanding, and I continue to remember stories of my childhood, my life, and my experiences.

PART TWO

Snippets

A Voice for My Mothers

Originally, I wanted to call this collection of writings "A Voice for My Mothers," but it was a lofty ambition, and my three mothers spoke too softly.

My mother is the woman who gave birth to me. She nurtured and taught me the art of living and surviving. Her voice trembled with regret, joy, sadness, and hope. Although, we do not see eye-to-eye on almost every issue nowadays, my mother taught me everything I know about how to be a strong woman.

Cambodia, my motherland, is the mother and caretaker of my ancestors. She is a mother of glories and atrocities. She has known peace and war, celebrating and suffering with her children, weeping in agony as she watched her fertile fields turned into the Killing Fields. Although Cambodia is no longer home, she continues to teach me what it means to be alive, to feel, love, and cry.

Mother Earth is a mother who desperately needs a voice. She has nurtured and fed the world with fruits from her blossoms. She is good and loving, tumultuous and unpredictable. Mother Earth, the entity of utmost beauty, is mother to all.

Giving a voice to my mothers promotes my own voice and its stories, which come in the form of fleeting thoughts, ideas, and distant memories. These stories are the schizophrenic voices in my head, begging to be told. I have written these stories many times, and each time I write, I project wisdom into my stream of consciousness. The memories are unchanging, yet each time I write, I am gifted with new insights into my past.

These stories represent my life in the refugee camps,

capturing the essence of how I lived then and how I carry my past with me in my life now. I write to scrutinize my experiences and understand my thoughts about the world, war and poverty, the struggle to survive and dwell with hope.

I live in a world that makes excuses. I make excuses, struggling to define my principles, only to realize that my decisions are based on emotion, not principle. I have neither the strength nor the desire to save the world, but I yearn to bring about some understanding between different peoples, no matter how insignificant it may seem.

I have played with the idea of Cambodia as a woman and a mother, expressing her in those terms. I think being seen as a mother is an honor and Cambodia has been loved as mothers would be loved. I have loved Cambodia even if my memories may have been the memories of others, and she continues to inspire me with hope and afflict me with despair.

My Mother's Garden

My mother has a green thumb, and whatever she plants grows beautifully. I take special delight in watching her garden grow. I cannot be a gardener because I do not have what it takes to tend a garden: to put in the time and effort to water it day by day until the plants grow, to patiently wait with anticipation and love.

One day I had an epiphany. Of course my mother is a great gardener; she was a farmer in Cambodia. Farming, growing, and tending gardens was her livelihood.

My mother's green thumb no longer seems special or unique. Many Khmer people grow wonderful gardens in their backyard and front yard. You can tell a Cambodian house by what is growing in their yard.

My mother made use of every space around the house. Her garden contains vegetables, fruits, and herbs that are used for cooking. Many Khmer people are flabbergasted by the concept of growing bushes and trees that do not produce edible fruits, unless they are shrubs that bring luck.

The trees and herbs that my mother planted at our old houses continue to flourish and feed the Khmer residents of our old neighborhoods.

Similarly, the fruit trees that she planted and tended before leaving Cambodia continue to feed our relatives.

Snippets

Hiding in my room and devouring historical romance novels, I dreamt of becoming a writer, writing about love and romance. I outlined plots for my novels and created titles and names for my heroes and heroines. But alas, my desire to be a historical romance writer was short-lived, but I still want to write.

• • •

My mother was not happy that I wanted to go away to college, but I was determined. I saw no point in arguing and merely watched her, debating with herself, presenting different reasons, pros and cons, though mostly cons. At the end of the conversation, she said to herself, "Fine, go. I have taught you right and wrong all of your life. If by now, you still do not know it, you will never know it. I do not want to be the reason that keeps you from going to the college of your choice and achieving your goals, so go ahead and go."

• • •

A Cambodian daughter who travels around the world
will give her parents a heart attack. My mother opposed
my plans to go abroad. I understood her concerns, but I
was determined to follow my dreams. At present, I have
traveled half way around the world and back many times.
My parents have finally accepted it and have even decided
to brag about their world-traveling daughter with pride,
"that daughter of mine has traveled far and wide and I do
not think she plans to settle down and have a family (husband) at all."

• • •

Last name, first name; here in America, it is written
first name, followed by last name, showing the importance
of the individual versus the collective. Phim, Navy. I was
Phim, Navy for the first nine years of my life, but I assimilated to America. I became Navy Phim. It was easier to as-
similate than to keep explaining that Phim is not my first
name and that in my country, last name is written first.

• • •

A child of refugee camps—what does it mean? As a child
of the refugee camps, I am well rounded. I know the Khmer
words of different provinces and regional dialects. For instance, MSG is *bejang* or *ma-sao-soup*. *Tirk-Kroung* or *Bok-
om-brouk*, two ways of saying the same thing depending
on your place of origin. One day, I came home and used a
word that was not commonly used in Battambang, Cambodia, and my relatives asked me, what part of Cambodia
are you from? I did not understand the question then, but
I finally have the answer. I am the product of the refugee camps, a no-man's land where Cambodians huddled
together, waiting to be saved. I came from a Cambodia
that shared the atrocities of the Killing Fields, surviving

in refugee camps and waiting to be rescued. I was rescued by America.

This Is Not A-Pot

Person A: *This is not A-Pot. Why do you have rice stashed away like that? This is Long Beach and the Khmer grocery store is around the corner. You can get a 50-pound bag of rice for $20.*

Person B: *Don't talk about things you don't understand. It is a survival mechanism of the intellects.*

Person A: *The intellects? Who would that be? You are nothing more than a starving student. Intellect, my ass.*

Person B: *There is a principle behind it.*

Person A: *Explain the principle to me again.*

Person B: *My roommate and I share the rice. I buy a bag and when we run out, he buys a bag. But when we run out of rice and it is his turn to buy it, he takes his sweet old time. In the meantime, I have no rice and I need my rice.*

Person A: *You are so Khmer.*

Person B: *I learned my lesson, so I stashed away some rice for emergency.*

Person A: *This is not A-pot but you are living in it.*

Person B: *Like you said, I'm a starving student. Living as though I'm in A-pot is a way of coping.*

Romeo's Father

Life in the refugee camps in Thailand and the Philippines prepared us for our life in the third country, our future home. There were opportunities to study English in the refugee camps for those who could afford it, and

it was mandatory that we attend English classes in the
Philippines.

Whenever we watched a movie in English, people with
better language comprehension translated it into Khmer
for us. I saw Franco Zefferelli's *Romeo and Juliet* in the
Philippines as a young child. It was in English and we had
translators helping us to understand the story. I remember the story quite well, a sad love story about lovers who
are kept apart because of poverty.

The people who translated the storyline did not know
English as well as they thought. In the part where Romeo visits the priest to make plans for his wedding, Romeo
calls the priest, "Father," but for lack of fluency in English
and cultural knowledge concerning priests, our translators thought the priest was Romeo's father. They thought
that Romeo and his father were poor people, and Romeo
could never marry Juliet because she came from a rich
family. In the end, they committed suicide because they
would rather die together than live without each other. It
was a sad story.

I saw the film again when I was in junior high. By
then, I understood every word. I knew the priest was not
Romeo's father and the star-crossed lovers of my childhood memories were changed, in a good way. Now I understand the story as it is meant to be understood.

I smiled, remembering the day I watched *Romeo and
Juliet* with a bunch of Khmer refugees, trying hard to understand Shakespeare's tragic story. I smiled, remembering the feeling of sympathy the audiences expressed for
Romeo, the poor young man who was living with his poor
father.

The translation was wrong, but they translated the
story so we would understand a story of love and poverty,
the refugees' story of *Romeo and Juliet*.

Family Name

Last name or family surname in Khmer is *chmoss jita*, which literally means "the name of grandfather." Thus, last names are not consistent or traceable within a Cambodian family. My last name would be the name of my grandfather on my father's side, and the last name of my children would be the last name of my husband's father. At least, this is how it works in my parents' province, Battambang. This custom may not be consistently practiced throughout Cambodia and Chinese-Cambodians probably follow a different tradition concerning last names.

Tro-Kole, the name of the family lineage, is another way of looking at last names within a Cambodian family. Some people follow this custom and keep their last name consistent within their family, mostly the rich (*sathei*) and the city dwellers. But for the farming population, last names do not play a role in daily life. They ask for the name of your grandfather to know who you are and what kind of family you belong to, to see if your family is honest or not.

In the refugee camps, people chose a last name for themselves in almost the same way that my birthday was chosen, randomly and inconsistently. My father gave me the same last name as his. My father's twin gave his children his first name as their last name.

The people who were hired by the United Nations to help with the translation and the paperwork to come to America decided on the spelling of our names. It was a difficult job but I think most of our names could have been spelled closer to the way they are pronounced. For instance, the *ch* sound in most Khmer names would have been better with a *j*, Janda instead of Chanda.

Some people ask me why I do not spell my first name

N-A-V-I-E. Would the *ie* make the *a* long? I did not have
a say in how it was spelled, but usually only one correc-
tion is necessary for people to then say my first name correctly.

The Color of Beauty

Mom: *Why are you so dark?*
Me: *Because you married a dark-skinned man.*
Mom: *"Koun-anh."*

My mother was speechless and did not utter any other
words, except for those two words, but those words were
packed with meaning. *Koun-anh,* my daughter. But she
said it to mean, *my daughter,* she is so difficult. *My daughter,*
look at how she talks to me. But luckily, my mother saw
it for what it was, a clever remark, and the conversation
ended with humor and a smile on both our faces.

I have heard it all of my life from relatives, family,
friends, and even strangers. *Kmao maleh, so dark.* But the
remark is loaded and really asks, why are you so dark? As
if I control it. Maybe I do because of the amount of sun I
exposed myself to, but I was born dark. Sometimes, it is
just a comment, *khmao maleh.* I'm not offended or insulted.
But it can be taken as an insult because Cambodian society
views light skin as the color of beauty. Thus, darkness, its
opposite, is unattractive. This is a common view within
Cambodia and many countries around the world.

Fortunately, I grew up in America with the black
revolutionary slogan "I'm black and I'm beautiful!" so my
skin color has little affect on my self-esteem even though
I know that some people see it as a hindrance to beauty.
But the light-skin-color mentality encompasses more than
beauty. Fair skin is also associated with class and the well

to do, those who do not labor away under the hot sun and have that early-aging darkness. The well to do in Cambodia were usually part Chinese, thus the light skin.

The color of beauty is an amusing dilemma at times, as with the exchange I had with my mother. For many people, this cultural bias translates into an internalized aversion of oneself. Many have been the butt of jokes and taunting and have been hurt, thus truly dislike this light-skin-color mentality. I have my own biases about skin color and beauty. I see pale, light skin as a sign of weakness belonging to the high-maintenance beauty queen. It is their bias when some see dark skin as a hindrance to beauty, and it is my bias when I see light skin as a sign of weakness, in the sense of having an inactive lifestyle. Being in California has probably influenced my view of attributing tan skin to people with an active and healthy lifestyle. Both biases are flawed, but the cultures we grow up in influence our outlook.

It is strange (but possibly fair) that you will see ugliness in the same people who judge you to be ugly based upon skin color and features that are different from theirs. In the end, I remind myself that it is merely a bias and a preference. I remember to judge people based on something more than their skin color and features.

Reahoo Jab Jan

On Groundhog Day, the groundhog comes out of his hole after a long winter of hibernation to look for his shadow and determine the weather for the next six weeks. If he sees his shadow, there will be another six weeks of winter, but if the day does not cast a shadow, the groundhog knows that spring is in the air and he stays outside. This concept was introduced to me in the movie *Ground-*

hog Day. The groundhog predicting the season reminded me of a Cambodian folk belief that the eclipse predicts the state of the world.

I am not sure if a solar eclipse has as much mystical power as a lunar eclipse, but Cambodians call the lunar eclipse *Reahoo Jab Jan*. *Reahoo* is a mythical demon and *Jan* is the moon. *Reahoo Jab Jan* can be translated as "Reahoo abducts the moon," a phrase that reminds me of "the rape of Persephone."

When *Reahoo Jab Jan* happens, it creates a commotion among the people of Cambodia. My experiences with the lunar eclipses and the way Khmer people celebrate them took place in the refugee camps. People go outside to bang pots and pans, trying to get *Reahoo* to release *Jan*.

It is also believed that if one sleeps through a lunar eclipse, one will become dim-witted. Thus, people wake up their young children, dragging them outside, half asleep, still rubbing their eyes to observe the astrological event reflected in a bowl of water, the proper way of observing this occurrence.

It is also a time ripe for making wishes and requests. Mostly, the request is for a prosperous harvest, good crops and an abundance of food. People tap on trees telling them to grow. I vaguely remember being half asleep and being tapped on my head by my uncle telling me to grow and to be endowed with intelligence.

There are three ways that *Jan* will be released from *Reahoo*. First, *Jan* emerges from the top, as if being spit out. Second, *Jan* materializes from the side, appearing to burst from *Reahoo's* chest. The third and final way is *Jan* sliding down from the bottom of *Reahoo*, signifying defecation.

As my mother related it to me, being spit out predicts a sickly state of the world, a world with diseases. Bursting out of the chest means the world will be prosperous with good harvests and plenty of food. The defecation of *Jan* shows that the world is facing an impoverished period.

Reahoo Jab Jan and Groundhog Day show how nature influences our lives, two different approaches from two different cultures to explain something similar.

Coining: Kaus Kjol

Kaus Kjol is a Cambodian practice used to chase illness away. *Kaus* means "to rub" and *kjol* means "the wind." The literal translation for *kaus kjol* would be "to rub the wind." But this translation does not explain the meaning behind the practice. An English term for this concept is "coining" or "dermabrasion" because it involves placing mentholated medicine or tiger balm on the skin and rubbing it with a coin until the skin turns red. There is a strict procedure as to which direction it is done and which part of the body is done first to chase the wind out in the appropriate direction and avoid aggravating the illness. When we came to America, my mother started using hand lotion instead of tiger balm as a lubricant for the coining, demonstrating how we adapt our practices to fit our new life, using the resources available at our fingertips, and showing how culture evolves and changes constantly. After the coining was done, my mother would rub tiger balm into the skin on our back or stomach. I love feeling the mentholated heat on my body and inhaling it to clear my sinuses.

I was raised on this method of healing. I hated it when I was younger, but *kaus kjol* as a healing method is part of my psyche. Whether or not it has a scientifically proven benefit, I cannot say. Maybe it is psychological, but I heal faster when I take medicines with coining.

Many Cambodian refugees from the first wave of migration were accused of child abuse because of the red marks left on children after coining. Nowadays, there are plenty of articles on coining. Most school counselors and health care professionals are educated about the practice, so mistaken accusations of child abuse no longer occur.

Mountains of Legends

It seems to me that the mountains of Cambodia are really molehills. I have not been everywhere in Cambodia and do not know enough about its mountain ranges to make a definitive statement, but as I traveled through the country and people pointed out different mountains to me, they did not look very mountain-like.

I love the mountains in my motherland because most seem to have a story or legend associated with them. For example, there is a legend and a story for *Phnom Sompoav* (Ship Mountain), *Phnom Krapeh* (Crocodile Mountain), and *Phnom Neang Kong-Rey, Phnom Pross, and Phnom Srey* (Male and Female Mountains).

Phnom Krapeh in Battambang is connected to a legend about a ship, a princess, and a dying crocodile that pounded his tail against the ground, breathing heavily in agony and causing two ponds to appear in front of him and another one behind him.

I was born in a village near *Phnom Krapeh*. I had the nickname *Krapeh* when I was younger because I bit a little girl on the nose. I bit her out of love. The Khmer word for it is *knanh*, like when you think a little baby is so adorable that you want to pinch her cheek. I thought she was so cute that I bit her, but it gave me a reputation as a biter, like a crocodile.

My mother has a special gift for legends and associations. She starts many sentences with "It seems." For instance, "It seems that you were born on that crocodile mountain rightly fit with your behavior." Or "Your name, if pronounced the American way, is associated with war and it seems appropriate for you, a baby born during war." I am saddened by this concept, "it seems appropriate for being born into a country of war." War is a heartbreaking event and should not be suitable for any situation, but it is the story of many lives.

The Uncle from Upstairs

~ yeh

Khmer people call each other by familial titles, "grandmother" and "grandfather," "aunt" and "uncle," "younger brother" or "older sister," as the case may be. These familial titles are respectable methods of addressing each other and are given according to age, when someone is at the age that qualifies them as a grandmother or an aunt. Names are rarely used. Married couples even address each other as "the mother of my children" or "the father of my children." Family friends usually address the person as "the mother of [name of the oldest child]." For instance, my mother is "the mother of A-Vy," (A-Vy is me). I have no idea what they called each other prior to their marriage and the existence of their children.

In the refugee camp, I lost my parents at a temple. As I panicked and cried, people stopped to help me. They asked for the names of my parents and I told them it was *mae* and *pok*, the Khmer words for mom and dad. During the commotion, my uncle happened to walk by and realized that I was the lost child, so he took me home.

I knew that names were rarely used and the respectable form of address was the familial title, but I did not know that it was considered rude to use someone's name, especially if you do not know each other well. During the period when my father was courting my mother, he would

mysteriously appear and cross her path. He offered to help
my mother carry whatever she was holding. One day, he
was quite forward and addressed her by her name (probably to show that he knew what it was). My mother was
offended and thought he was a rude person, but his per-
sistence paid off.

It is not to say that names are not used at all. They
have to be used after the familial title, for example, "Aunt
Jen." For most of us, we have to use the names to distin-
guish which aunts or uncles we are addressing since there
are so many of them. But with family friends, I only call
them "aunt" and "uncle" with no name attached. In most
cases, I do not even know their name, especially because I
have only heard my parents call them "the mother of so-
and-so."

When I moved into a new apartment, I met the upstairs neighbor and we had a few conversations. I called
him "uncle," as dictated by custom. He is around my father's age, and I knew that I would probably never know
his name. I think of him as the "uncle from upstairs."

One day, the mailman mistakenly put our mail in his
box. He brought it down and put it outside our door with
a note explaining that the mailman had mistakenly put it
in the wrong box. He signed it, "the uncle from upstairs"
(*poo nov ler*). I laughed. The uncle from upstairs was not
just a name that I secretly used; it is a name that he signed
on his letter to us.

Fragments and Bits

English has become the language of my thoughts, my
expressions, and my remembrances. I relive different memories and conversations in English even though I experienced them in Khmer. I write them in English but when

I try to remember them in Khmer, the exact words and phrases do not come. The sentences and syntaxes, what were they? This seems to be part of the normal process of assimilation to my identity as a Cambodian-American.

• • •

There are many chaotic memories involving food and my life as a refugee. In Sakeo, my aunt saw a snake that created uproar within our neighborhood and nearby neighborhoods as people gathered together to hunt it. I do not know what kind of snake it was or if they hunted it to protect us or for food, but we feasted on it, sharing it with most of the community, but particularly with the people who killed it.

In the Philippines, there was an incident involving food and hunting that has lingered in my memory and served as a basis for many of my experiences as a world traveler. My father and uncles went into the mountain to find food, which included gathering crickets and poaching honeycomb. They were brave hunters, but one of my uncles, the baby of the family, was badly injured from the expedition. They poked and probed at the honeycomb and the bees attacked in defense. In trying to escape the attack, my uncle tumbled down the mountain. He was brought home injured and my grandmother reprimanded my father and uncles for not taking better care of him.

The crickets and honeycomb provided us with a feast, but my injured uncle was not able to enjoy it. I remember the savory taste of the roasted crickets with peanuts stuffed inside. During my travels, I have tasted crickets from different countries, trying to capture the taste of my childhood memories. There are differences in taste and style of preparation. I had them in Thailand and they were deep fried whole with no peanuts inside. I had them in Mexico, soaked in lemon and chili.

PART THREE

Embrace

Srok Khmer

Have you been back to *Srok Khmer*? *Srok* means country. *Srok Khmer* is a phrase that describes the motherland. *Srok Khmer*, the country of Khmer. The question is used to gauge a person's affinity to the motherland. Has this person followed their heart's desire and returned for a visit or many visits? This person has returned many times while that person has no desire to visit, *ever*. This other person wants to visit but has been afraid of the emotions buried deep within.

I have visited the motherland four times. My first trip lasted from October to December of 1998. I visited again at the end of 1999 through the beginning of 2000. I returned for the third time as 2004 ended and 2005 began and for the fourth time in January 2006.

Before my third trip, I was asked, "Why Cambodia? Why do you keep going back?" I was stunned by the nature of the question. I was bombarded with a billion thoughts. First of all, I was not making a yearly visit like some lucky people, and there was a big gap since my last trip. Despite the rush of emotions and words, I was unable to express myself. I did not want to answer, because if the question had to be asked, the answer would most likely appear to be frivolous. The kind of love, heartache, and pain I feel for *Srok Khmer* is deeply imbedded within my soul; these feelings are suffused with glorious memories and stories that are real, even if they are stories and distant memories that may not even be mine.

The person who asked me the question took her first trip to Cambodia that coincides with my third visit. We did not meet up, but on her return, she poignantly reflected on her trip, and I knew then that she had answered her own question.

Cambodia: A Dying Saga

Cambodia is a land whose history rivals the history of the world and the myths of the Greek gods and goddesses. She has her own history and myths. She is a mother that provides a cradle for life, a womb for births, and a chamber for deaths. Her terrain has been substantiated with the sweat and toil of her children. Their ashes and essences, ghostly remnants, their laughter, pain, and suffering are incorporated into her energy and greatness. The vibrations of love and pain pulsate through her like the blood that courses through my veins.

Cambodia is a relic of the Khmer Empire, its warriors, and god-kings. The ancestors of Cambodia fought, conquered, and built monuments to honor their gods, acting in accordance with other great warriors and empires and rivaling the Aztecs, Incas, Egyptians, Romans, and Greeks. The remains of these gloating, religious monuments are left for her progeny to admire, spurring inner pride and anger for the greatness that was lost. The Khmer Empire, with its conquering and its defeats on an evolutionary timescale, demonstrates Darwin's theory of evolution and the "survival of the fittest." Cambodia has played the role of the fierce warrior, the unstoppable entity, but today she is a frail piece of land. She has become smaller and smaller from the encroachment of her neighbors. Sadly, she has become weakened and is now an insignificant realm because her children continue to bicker, shredding her body apart piece by piece.

Cambodia's myths of the Naga princess, the heavenly dancers known as *Apsara*, the churning of the milk, and the elixir of life rival the Greek myths of Persephone, Her-cules, and Achilles. Cambodia is a tragedy and an *Odyssey*. She is a parody, mimicking the plotlines of the great dra-mas and betrayals.

Cambodia is a land haunted by blood and death. She is sad and pitiful, a beauty that breaks hearts, but she is worthy of desire and aspiration.

I was born into a nest infested with war, dressed in nakedness.

Cambodia offers beauty and swaying palm trees, but I was swept away from her bosom on a journey to find peace and healing, away from a saga that lingers.

Homing Beacon

Cambodia is my homing beacon, although it has not been home for a long time. I attend the call of Cambodia to fulfill an inner yearning of the soul. In Cambodia, I am a stranger who is uncomfortable with the temperament of the land and the nature of the people. I leave Cambodia and return to America to find the comfort of home, a place whose disposition I understand. I am home in Cambodia and home in America, but America is the home of comfort. I feel safe in it.

Cambodia is the home of memories, the taste and scent of tropical fruits, the call of childhood. Cambodia is home to the colors of simple sarongs and sophisticated silks.

I attend to the calls of Cambodia, but I have also left her behind like a mistress who has satisfied her lover.

California is a home that provides many reasons to disregard Cambodia, but Cambodia is not easily forgotten. Songs and phrases of hope make me think of Cambodia and what she can have one day.

The Colors of Sarong in Cambodia

Color me Khmer with sarong. Color me woman with sarong. I feel feminine and soft when I wear sarong. Having lived more than a quarter of a century, and having lived to an age where most women are married and have children, I still struggle with the responsibility of being an adult. I feel like a girl instead of a woman, but when I wear sarong, I feel like a woman. I feel like a Khmer woman.

Across Cambodia, the colors of sarongs contrast with the colors of the rice paddies, like palm trees and tropical fruits, signifying the tastes and colors of Cambodia. Women dress in floral-patterned sarongs in hues of red, blue, purple, green, yellow, and orange, exploding with soothing designs and decorations steeped in myth. *Khmer Sarong* is the color of defiant beauty and femininity.

Young girls wear sarongs with elastic at the waist, but women wear sarongs without elastic, *sarong boht*, which are simply folded and tucked to the side. When I became a woman, I was given a sarong without elastic, but among the many sarongs I have today, I still have one with elastic. I switch back and forth between girlhood and womanhood depending on my mood. Wearing *sarong boht* properly and keeping it from falling requires skill, talent, and experience.

Sarongs are worn by all Khmer people, young and old, male and female, residing in the city and in the countryside. Cambodian men wear a special type of sarong called *sarong soht*.

Sarong, for Khmer people, has many purposes and life stages. I love the colors of *Khmer Sarong*; their vivid hues scattered throughout Cambodia, swaying in the wind and rain, along dusty roads and rice fields. They paint Cambodia with beauty and simplicity.

Swimwear

Create beautiful, stylish swimwear with a sarong. Pull it to your chest and turn it into a bathing suit. Most Khmer women who live in the countryside bathe outside, near their home or in a body of water, wearing sarongs. The "sarong bathing suit" is reserved and modest compared to the bikini, but it is more sensual.

In Cambodian culture, modesty influences clothing, people dress in a way that does not call attention to themselves. In my America, in the state of California, our apparel seems to ask for attention, people dress to look and feel sexy. This contrast can be seen in the swimsuits worn by Cambodians and Americans. When it comes to my swimsuit, I prefer the Cambodian style, a suit modestly covering as much as possible.

How does modesty become a part of one's psyche? I grew up hearing about the need for modesty from my mother and relatives and I bought into it. "Cover up." "Do not show too much skin." "These American, they have no shame!" (a comment in response to someone wearing a bikini).

In the locker room of my junior high, I was unnerved to see people changing in front of me without a care for modesty. I changed my clothes in a way that showed very little. Overtime, I became immune to people changing and walking around naked in front of me. I do not view nakedness negatively, but I still prefer to change privately. I still wear modest swimsuits these days, but my modesty asserts my Khmer sensibility. It prevents me from walking around in a skimpy bathing suit or changing in the nude in front of other women, but I accept my modesty as a natural part of me and my identity, a mixture of two values, American and Khmer.

Sampot Khmer

The image of an ideal Khmer beauty: a woman dressed in a traditional outfit, a *sampot* and *aw-pak*. *Sampot* means skirt. *Aw-pak* is an embroidered shirt. A sarong is a particular type of *sampot* that is worn everyday as people go about their daily chores and lives. The *sampot* is made from silk, which is worn for special-occasions like attending a religious ceremony at a temple or a wedding.

This ideal of feminine beauty is going to the temple, carrying the food that she will offer to the monks, and a parasol to protect her from the sun. She is elegance, beauty, and softness.

The word *traditional* makes it seem like something so long ago and far away. But these outfits, the *sampot* Khmer and *aw-pak*, were a part of my life as I was growing up, dressing in traditional outfits for the temple and weddings.

I love Khmer outfits. I feel feminine and beautiful in them (the same way I feel in sarongs) and I always seize the opportunity to dress in them.

I had my first Khmer outfit made when I was in ninth grade and it fits me to this day because my mother had the prudence to make it a size or so bigger. Prior to that day, I had many Khmer outfits in my closet but they were all hand-me-downs from my aunts.

I love Khmer silks, soft and smooth, almost perfect. My friends and I used to tailor evening gowns from Khmer silks for weddings and parties. Even when we were not wearing traditional Khmer outfits, we were wearing something that was Khmer. Almost everybody in the Cambodian community wore gowns made from Khmer silks, feeling beautiful in our traditional fabric.

Nowadays, my trips to the temple have lessened considerably, especially since I live on my own. I do not have a mother at home to take me to the temple and tell me what to do and how to behave according to different religious ceremonies. But once a year on Khmer New Year, I feel inspired to go to the temple. On that day I take out my Khmer outfits and put one on.

History in Colors

The color of a sarong reflects the history of its life. Color fades from a sarong that has been worn and washed for many years. My cousin, who is a poor farmer in Cambodia, has a sarong with faded color, but I can imagine the luster of its color when she first bought it. In her life, she does not have the luxury of throwing away a sarong that has faded to the color of a rag. She will wear it for the rest of her life and she may even pass it down to other members of the family. She may find another purpose for it, using it as a wrap for a newborn baby or cutting it up for baby clothes.

The fading color signifies the age of a sarong but not its death.

During the 2005 New Years Parade in Long Beach, Khmer women wore new sarongs with vibrant colors.

The life of a sarong is written in its color. A faded sarong has lived the life of its owner, traversing many roads and rice paddies. It has been washed in rivers, and its color has seeped into the earth of Cambodia.

Embracing Freedom

For the first six years in America, I grew up with an extended family, living in the same house with my aunts,

uncles, their children, and my grandmother. I was told
from left and right what to do, how to act, walk, dress, and
cut my vegetables. I never had a moment to myself.

After high school, I moved out of the house and lived
on my own. I became independent, adjusting to and em-
bracing the silence. I have experienced both situations. I
am Khmer and American.

The importance of the collective and the individual is
valued differently for Cambodians and Americans. I have
assimilated independence, and give it great value at this
point in my life, asserting my American identity.

The first time I slept away from home, away from my
family, was the summer I graduated from high school.
I had to attend a three-day orientation at UCLA before
starting school there that fall. I missed my family. Three
days felt like three years. I had so much time to myself, to
think, reflect, and waste—time that used to be spent with
my family, doing something or doing nothing together.

I was thrilled when the orientation came to an end.
I was ready to go home and be with my family, to fight
over what TV show to watch, to watch them together, and
laugh together.

I walked out of the dorm into the sunlight, adjusting
my eyes to its brightness before scanning the parked cars.
I saw my father's car and noticed that my whole family
was in the car, sitting there, waiting for me.

I smiled. They had missed me as much as I had missed
them. Instead of waiting for my father to bring me home,
they all came to get me. I still smile when I remember that
day.

After college graduation, I moved back home, but
within a year, I moved out again, to be on my own and
live an independent life. I chose to live and embrace different aspects of my personality, tastes and values that are
particularly Khmer or American. Living on my own and

being independent is the assertion of my American personality.

There are moments of loneliness that remind me to visit my family, especially when I have taken my independence to the extreme and have forgotten to enjoy the merriment of having a family and being with them.

Cambodian Splendor

My mother's long, thick, black, semi-wavy hair was her trademark in her younger days. She symbolizes the beauty and splendor of the Cambodian woman. My mother provides glimpses into the lives of Cambodian women with the simple care she puts into herself.

She oils her hair with Indian coconut oil to make it shiny, shaping my image of beauty and femininity. My own hair has always been as black as night and almost as long. In high school when everyone dyed their hair blonde and streaked it red, I dyed mine black. When everyone was changing their hairstyle, I kept mine the same—long and simple, tied in a ponytail. After many years of being known as the girl with the long hair, I cut it short during college. I was ready to try a different hairstyle—something that did not fit the traditional Khmer idea of femininity and beauty.

My family, grandmother, aunts, and uncles have always been blunt about the shortcomings of my looks, but my long hair somewhat compensated for my deficiencies. When I cut my hair, I lost everything that was beautiful.

My mother has tried to instill the concept of *looking* and caring about the way I look and dress. In her younger days, she was fashionable and a sight for sore eyes. Being beautiful means avoiding the sun, and the sacrifice is too much for me. When I was younger, I loved being outside.

Nowadays, I enjoy the outdoors and being a part of nature even more as a way to escape the frenzied city life. I turn many shades darker during the summer but I do not mind because I get it from enjoying life.

Cambodia is the motherland—but my mother, the woman who gave birth to me, is my Cambodia. She tells me stories of the motherland that nurture my love and connection to Cambodia. She represents Cambodia and its women with all her beauty and splendor.

During my first trip back, my mother's brothers and sisters gave me a tour of the rice fields, using terms unique to rice farming as if I could understand them. I walked around nodding as if I understood. They showed me a mango tree that my mother had planted. It was a foot high when my family left Cambodia, but now it towers more than fifteen feet high.

I walked around feeling sweaty and dusty from the heat and the dirt road. I marveled at the idea of looking and feeling "beautiful" as my mother did in the sweltering heat and dusty village where feeling clean and fresh seems impossible. But as I walked on the ground of my mother's motherland, I was privy to a greater understanding of my mother, her past and life.

Young Merchants of Cambodia

The sight of children touting products at tourist sites is common in Cambodia (and many other parts of the world). I have a love-hate relationship with the young merchants of Cambodia. They can be frustrating, shoving their products in your face when you want to enjoy the serenity and beauty of Angkor. They are only trying to make a living, but I still find it hard to relinquish my irritation.

These young merchants have amazing language skills

and can converse with tourists in English, French, and Japanese with a great deal of fluency. They are intelligent, resourceful business people.

As I walked into the temple at Rolous, these young merchants trailed behind me, echoing, "Madam, would you like to buy a scarf?" After I said no, they continued to trail behind me, but they gave me my space by staying a few paces behind.

Once I finished looking over the structure, I engaged in a conversation with them, asking where they lived and how they learned to speak English. They told me about a teacher who offered free English classes. As they talked to me, they forgot about their status as merchants and happily shared their stories, enjoying a little rest.

I asked them for a photo and they were happy to oblige. Once I was ready to leave, they reverted to being merchants and asked in unison, "Madam, would you like to buy a scarf?"

Khmer Features

The perception of those who see themselves as different is a good starting point in discussing Khmer features. Chanrithy Him, who is Chinese-Cambodian, provides a description of the differences between herself and "pure Cambodian" in her autobiography, "When Broke Glass Floats." She describes her Cambodian neighbor as "pure" and "cultured," with "dark skin and large eyes." Khmer eyes can be large, round, and beautiful. The dark skin is a noticeable difference between "pure" Cambodians and Chinese-Cambodians, but the skin tone of Cambodians ranges from light brown to extremely dark. "Curly black hair, flat noses, full lips, and dark chocolate skin" can describe Khmer features, but these are merely possible features, not exclusively Khmer features. Khmer features include flat and sharp noses, curly hair and straight hair, full lips and thin lips, dark chocolate skin and lighter tone of brown, large eyes or almond eyes.

The legend of the origin of Cambodia captures the diversity that exists in the features of Cambodians. We are the offspring of a Naga princess and an Indian prince, a foreigner exiled from his homeland who encountered and fell in love with the Naga princess during his travels. The land of Cambodia was a gift from the Naga king. *Srok Khmer* is a nation that begins with a union between the power and spirit of the land and a foreigner, which can be seen in the influence of Indian culture on Cambodia. Many of us who consider ourselves to be Khmer, the descendents of the foreign prince and the Naga princess, have been mistaken for other ethnicities and these include Pacific Islander, Samoan, Hawaiian, Filipino, Indonesian, Malaysian, Indian, Middle Eastern, and many more. Some have even been asked if they are partly African. When I traveled, I was able to pass as a local in the towns of many countries, including Thai, Indian, Burmese, and Nepali. In Latin America, I was mistaken as indigenous. Khmer features incorporate half of the world if not more.

Drunken Conversation

Person A: *You bourgeoisies are the ones that destroyed Cambodia with your decadent lifestyle and obese bellies. You exploited the poor of our nation for your perverse desires.*

Person B: *You poor peasants are the ones who destroyed Cambodia with your ignorance and superstitions. You were easily led and easily controlled.*

Person A: *You are the stock of corruption.*

Person B: *You are the stock of ignorance.*

Person C: *Which side am I on? I am neither bourgeoisie nor peasantry. My father was a teacher, not a farmer, but he also raised pigs to supplement our livelihood.*

Person B: *Which side did your father fight on during the war?*

Person C: *We were civilians throughout the war.*

Person A: *Both of my parents, aunts, and uncles fought in the Khmer Republican Army.*

Person B: *My father was the general of the Khmer Republican Army.*

Person A: *Your father was the corrupt official who never saw the frontline.*

Person B: *Who writes our history? The general or some foot soldiers?*

Person A: *Every perspective counts and needs to be accounted for.*

Person B: *You are so naive.*

Person A: *You are so arrogant.*

This was a drunken conversation between friends. Imagine if it was between foes.

PART FOUR

The Journey

A Hyphenated Identity

I am a child of the refugee camps. I lived in different refugee camps in Thailand from 1979 to 1983, in Kao-I-Dang, Sakeo, and Transit. The Khmer pronunciation for Transit is "trong-seat" and that is how the word has lived in my head and that is how I remember it to this day, even though I know its real pronunciation and meaning. Transit is *"the act of passing over, across, or through; passage."* The way Cambodians view their fate in refugee camps is akin to being in limbo, waiting to be cleansed in purgatory before being sent to heaven. They talked about waiting for the opportunity to be sent to the "third country," a new place, and a new level of existence, where gold and money are found on the street—the land of opportunity—America. In those transitional refugee camps—our purgatory—we were given shots and immunizations *to be purified* of disease.

I am a refugee seeking refuge. I was tossed across many miles of ocean arriving in America from the Philippines in 1984, when I was nine years old. America was my refuge, but at nine I thought of it as a temporary sanctuary. I had listened to people in the camps, including my parents, reminiscing passionately and lovingly about Cambodia, promising that someday they would return to their birth country. I was captivated with stories of that amazing land and the remarkable love they have for it. I was also planning to return to *Srok Khmer,* when the glory of peace and grandeur of the olden days resumed. At my elementary school, when I encountered racism, and the cruelty of children telling me I should go back to where I came from, I thought to myself, "Yes, someday, I will return to my beloved *Srok Khmer*, my homeland, my birthplace."

After ten years in America, I noticed that I was thinking in English. I no longer translated Khmer into English before speaking. English had become my preferred form of expression; America had become home. During my first trip abroad in 1996, I introduced myself as Cambodian-American. I no longer plan to permanently return to Cambodia, and I have finally accepted that I am Cambodian-American. Being Cambodian alone did not explain who I am to the people I met abroad who wanted to understand my cultural background. I had to acknowledge what America has given me and that I was now a hyphenated American.

But I *am* Khmer. *Khmer* can stand alone by itself; *American* has to be preceded by something more descriptive, because although I am American, *my soul feels poetically Khmer.* The past twenty years have been a process of assimilating, eliminating, and accepting different aspects of the Khmer and American cultures. The question of my identity is constantly raised by Khmer, Cambodian-Americans, other Americans, and people generally. I answer by looking inward and outward at my experiences, present and past, and then say I am Khmer or Cambodian-American.

Stupid American-Born

Stupid American is a phrase that echoes in many regions of the world. Stupid, stupid. Americans are the stupidest people in the world, they say, but people around the world want to come to America. People around the world say they hate Americans. What can we say? To be loved and hated is the true measure of stardom.

Stupid American-born. These are my three siblings who were born in America.

When my sister saw our picture from Kao-I-Dang, she exclaimed in shock, "You guys were in jail?" It was a picture of the whole family with my father holding a number to identify us. It does look like a family mug shot. And the refugee camp *was* a jail in many aspects. Her innocent comment was insightful, almost a bull's-eye on the truth.

My American-born siblings know so little of what went on in Cambodia. They were never a part of it like I was. Even though I was merely an infant, I grew up in it, heard about it, and can relate to it. But my American-born siblings need to learn about it and gain their own understanding of where their parents and older sister and brother came from, a war-torn country.

I am the smallest and shortest in our family, and the running joke is that I did not get enough to eat while growing up. It is a joke with a seed of truth. There are differences between myself and my American-born siblings: our sizes, views, understandings, coping mechanisms, the assimilation of our identities, and how we cope and fight with our parents.

In time, I hope my American-born siblings will want to gain a better understanding of where we came from, why we left, and what it means to be in America, to have freedom and peace, to live and die with dignity, with none of the horror that so many people have experienced elsewhere in the world.

The Journey

My family left Cambodia because of war and upheaval: for many years my knowledge was too limited to explain this statement. It was a stated fact that I took for granted. I remembered my life and experiences in the refugee camps and snippets of stories about the war, but I was ignorant of the minor and major details that contributed to the warfare in Cambodia. Different stories only supplied pieces to an incomplete puzzle.

When I saw the movie *The Killing Fields* in 1984, I was in junior high. An interested teacher asked me about the war in Cambodia. He must have seen the movie the same night I did. He talked about the horror of the Khmer Rouge regime and asked if I had relatives who were murdered for having an education. I did not know that educated people were targeted for murder, and I did not grasp the implications of the question.

My embarrassment did not force me to learn about it. The movie repressed my desire to know more. By the time I was in college, it was harder to remain ignorant. The movie shows the horror people experienced under a fanatical communistic leadership with schizophrenic policies and a merciless disregard for human life; the movie portrays only a fraction of what is necessary to understand the civil war in Cambodia.

My first visit to Cambodia provided some insights into the life of Cambodians and the heartbreaking reality of working, dreaming, and breathing in a war-torn country that is far from healed. I had heard of corruption and exploitation of the poor, but I still did not understand the intricacies of Cambodian politics and the selfishness that undermines the beautiful spirit of her people. I began conversing with people about life and politics and the puzzle pieces slowly began to fall into place. I read, analyzed, listened, discussed, and argued with others with heated passion.

I have always felt in tune with my Khmer identity and culture. I live with it, fight against it, and work with it. I spoke Khmer at home until I went away to college. I can cook most of the Khmer dishes from my parents' region of Battambang. I understand and employ the necessary form of respect with adults. I am soothed by Khmer melodies. I was part of the refugee experience. I grew up in Long Beach, California, the city with the largest Cambodian population in the United States. I am surrounded by Khmer friends who share my experiences and disillusionment, banding together to revive hope for ourselves, our culture, and our people. There have been many ill-fated attempts to create, inspire, and unite our shattered identities. Internet communities, forum discussions, literary journals, and other types of websites have sprung out of our desire to heal and educate ourselves and others. I was an enthusiastic part of this movement, creating and maintaining different websites, searching for stories of inspiration to share with the Cambodian community. Despite my encounters with inspirational people, events, and situations, there were disheartening incidences, like the sex trade, which have affected my interest in Cambodia, her tragic history, and brilliant endeavors causing me to be selective about what I want to know.

My journey to understand the history of Cambodia began in 2000. The story of war in Cambodia cannot end with history books. My soul needs to be fed inspirational stories of survival. I want to know that we have survived and can share messages of hope. In 2000, I began to read different autobiographies of survivors of the Killing Fields.

Autobiographies that I highly recommend are *A Cambodian Odyssey* by Haing Ngor; *When Broken Glass Floats* by Chanrithy Him; *Stay Alive, My Son* by Pin Yathay; and *Music Through the Dark* by Bree Lafreniere. *A Cambodian Odyssey* may be the definitive autobiography on the Killing Fields because it includes descriptions of life before the war and the journey across the border to Thailand and

America. *When Broken Glass Floats* reminds me of what it means to be Khmer, growing up with stories of magic hidden in the Himalayas. *Stay Alive, My Son* contains a stoic, yet powerful view of survival, while *Music Through the Dark* is strangely disturbing and beautiful. I have some of these books on my shelf at home and when a friend wants to read an autobiography of a survivor of the Killing Fields, I offer them one of my favorites.

Cambodia's children have come a long way, trekking across their homeland, becoming refugees in Thailand, and dispersing across the world to countries offering asylum. The world knows about the Killing Fields and the atrocities in Cambodia.

I struggle with the history of Cambodia and the evil we have unleashed on each other. I need to educate myself for healing and understanding. I need answers. How can people be so evil? How do they live with themselves? I want to know about their remorse, shame, and guilt. I have even resorted to reading the autobiography of Kheiv Samphan, one of the prominent leaders among the Khmer Rouge, through a book club, but we did not get far. I was unable to understand the political terms in the book. I read *Becoming Evil: How Ordinary People Commit Genocide and Mass Killing* by James Waller to gain insight into the human mind and the dynamics of atrocity. This is a powerful book to accompany the stories of Cambodia.

My journey has led me to the painful knowledge that the Khmer Rouge have not taken responsibility for their acts of brutality. They claimed to be ignorant of the crimes against humanity; the closest admission of transgression was a statement by Nuon Chea, "Brother Number Two," asserting that in such situations, there will be mistakes. The Khmer Rouge followers in Pailin denied of any personal knowledge of the Killing Fields, stating that they had heard of it but did not see it firsthand. Some even prayed to Pol Pot as a revered ancestor for protection. In their case, I have come to terms with their life of limitation, their lack of opportunity and knowledge beyond propaganda. However, among my colleagues and my generation, it is not about believing that the atrocities happened, but whether or not we care to know and make the time to educate ourselves and begin the journey toward healing and understanding of one's past.

The Question

What kind of country and people would allow the Killing Fields to occur? I have read this question in books and heard it during presentations. Sometimes, it has been asked rhetorically. There was a time in my life when I thought, "What a stupid question! Why are they asking about the people and the country? Only a group of monsters would be capable of doing what the Khmer Rouge did. It was not a whole nation of people that allowed it or participated in it!"

But this is the ultimate question raised not only by the Killing Fields but also by Cambodian history and my past. I am no longer satisfied with shaking my fist at the gods and pushing the atrocities to the back of my mind.

Prior to the Khmer Rouge victory in 1975, the time was ripe for revolution. The communist superpowers wanted to spread communism, and America wanted to contain it. In neighboring Vietnam, for example, the Americans and the south Vietnamese were fighting the communist revolutionaries. Years earlier, Cambodian students studying abroad were introduced to Marxism and leaned toward it. These obscure intellectuals became the leaders of the Khmer Rouge. The Viet Minh, Hồ Chí Minh's revolutionary national liberation movement, and the Chinese government also assisted in giving life to the Khmer Rouge, and their strength was further increased when Prince Sihanouk joined them to fight against the government that overthrew him.

Communism, for all its flaws, is rooted in the fight for equality. Lawlessness, exploitation, and corruption were a part of life in Cambodia among society's upper echelon, which generally treated people below them as subhuman. This corruption still exists today, with the intimidation to pay bribes at airports and many other places. Subjection to cruelty and humiliation continue to mar the life of the poor. I have seen it during my visits to Cambodia. The well-to-do still persist in treating their servants with cruelty. Yelling and cursing at them in front of guests seems to be the norm. The concept of human dignity is not commonly accepted.

Khiev Samphan was a member of parliament before his disappearance and later reemergence as a Khmer Rouge leader. He spoke against corruption and refused to take bribes. For daring to speak against corruption, he was stripped and beaten after a meeting. He could have been recorded as an admirable, honest figure in the history books, but there was no room for greatness and great men in Cambodia. He was admired for his principles, but he became part of a regime that can never be forgiven. People who spoke against the ill practices of Cambodia, like Samphan, were chased into the jungle to become monsters.

Is it hard to see how and why such extreme cruelty would occur in the Killing Fields? Cambodian society has long been guided by the notion that those in power may treat those under them as they please. The Khmer Rouge was pushing for a classless society, implementing policies to eradicate all enemies or suspected enemies, including their own members.

We can argue that revenge and jealousy on the part of the poor compelled extreme cruelty in the Killing Fields. We can argue that it was their ignorance that made them easy to brainwash for the bidding of *Angka*, the organization that is the Khmer Rouge. I have heard these arguments and accede that these are valid points, but these are not the only reasons for the Killing Fields. Accepting these as the sole reasons for the cruelty and existence of the Killing Fields has erased our accountability. I have heard the contention that ignorant farmers with their superstitious beliefs about royal blood joined the Khmer Rouge, fighting on the wrong side for a wrong cause. At the outset of the war, there was no right or wrong side. There were people who despised communism. There were people who were disillusioned with the corruption and exploitation of the Lon Nol government (this concept was discussed in Bophana, a film by Rithy Panh). There were people who wanted certain rights and society kept these from them. It was not only the ignorant, uneducated farmers who admired what the Khmer Rouge was fighting for (this concept is discussed in *Stay Alive, My Son*).

The phrase *ignorant, uneducated farmers* is explosively biased. How is education defined? Is it limited to being literate with a college degree? What about critical thinking skills and the ability to contribute to society and function with the resources given to you? Literacy is high among the rich people in Cambodia, as in most countries, but the percentage of literacy for the rest of Cambodia, who happened to be poor farmers, is significantly smaller. I am reluctant to use the term *educated* because the supposedly educated people in Cambodia do not bestow upon others their right to a life of dignity. They do not know what it means to treat others like human beings. An "educated person" is still ignorant, if he or she has never learned to

treat others like human beings. Cambodia needs education
for all members of her society, the educated rich and the
uneducated poor.

Lastly, people who can easily divide the country into
the educated and the uneducated are not looking at the
bigger picture. The two sides of the war were not divided
into the uneducated peasants against educated bourgeoisie.
The peasants, both illiterate and literate, were part of the
Lon Nol Army. Most of the leaders of the Khmer Rouge
were literate, educated individuals. Pol Pot himself was a
teacher, and some were former members of parliament.
Many factors contribute to the tragedy of Cambodia, and
that tragedy is the fault of the society as a whole, not any
one group of people. It is easy to blame the rich for their
decadent lifestyle and immoral behavior and the poor for
their superstition and ignorance. It may be more prudent
to look at the society and our own actions and how we
contributed to the atrocities (the actions of our parents, if
not our own). The rich and the poor, the uneducated and
educated, are part of this society that was capable of the
atrocities of the Killing Fields.

Were Your Parents Khmer Rouge?

"Were your parents Khmer Rouge?" I was stunned by
this question from an e-mail correspondent. My parents
were not *Khmer Kraharm*. They were never a part of that
movement before, during, or after. They were farmers
working the land, living in blissful ignorance until the war
infiltrated their village and farmland.

My mother was the youngest in her family, the only
unmarried daughter left during the war. She was living
with my grandmother in her hut. My father was a friend of
my mother's cousin, who aspired to be a matchmaker. He

brought my father to my mother's house and introduced them. It was love at first sight for my father. From that day onward, he would "accidentally" cross her path on the road near her village. One day, he finally asked my mother if she would accept his proposal if his family should come to ask for her hand in marriage. My mother said yes, and they were married. A year later, I was born.

Prior to meeting my mother, my father was a monk. The truth be told, my father was not a brave man with any lofty ambition of fighting for Cambodia. He chose the temple to escape the war. Three years later, after he had received enough education as a monk, he left the temple to become a layman. A year later, he met and fell in love with my mother.

My parents were too busy with courtship, marriage, and farming, surviving the chaos of war, and starting a family to be involved with the Khmer Rouge. My e-mail correspondent and I had been discussing the responsibility of accurately representing the tragedy of the Killing Fields. I think a book that presents the tragedy of Cambodia incorrectly is a disservice to the people of Cambodia, but he felt that, despite inaccurate information, a book that brings attention to the Killing Field has merit.

His question may have been a deflection from our heated discussion, but I grew up hating the Khmer Rouge, so it was offensive to even be asked that question. I have always wondered, "How do we both punish and forgive the Khmer Rouge?"

The Flute Player is a documentary film about Arn Chorn-Pond, a human rights activist and gifted musician, who survived the Killing Fields. The most poignant moment for me in the film was when Arn questioned his own humanity and actions as a young Khmer Rouge soldier. He was a teenager during the Khmer Rouge regime and like many teenagers, he was forced into the Khmer Rouge

Army to spy on people. If nothing else, the film is good for the mental health of the Cambodian community. We must have many people who are remorseful for what they did, living with pain and guilt; but of course, there are those who are not remorseful.

It was an interesting question to ponder: what if my parents were Khmer Rouge? What would they have taught me about the war? How would I see the world? How would I view forgiveness? Would I and could I forgive them? One simple question that started a million more: "Were your parents Khmer Rouge?"

Misplaced and Displaced

I accept hatred and anger of the Khmer Rouge as valid. I spent years hating them myself, and I did not have family members that were killed by their regime. Both of my parents survived the Killing Fields, and I will always be grateful for that. I can never adequately express my sympathy for my country and the world. I cannot think about the senseless killing without feeling unsettled and queasy—to know what we have done to each other in the form of genocides, the Holocaust, the Killing Fields, and the recent beheadings in the Middle East.

I spent years hating the Khmer Rouge and Hitler for the sake of humanity. I have tried to find the silver lining in the existence of human beings. I have dared to ask, "So what if the world comes to an end?" Let it end, and with it, the legacy of horrors.

Religious and philosophical perspectives, life experience, and many discussions have contributed to my acceptance of the world, allowing me to look and see what is good and decent, as well as what is evil and despairing. In the end, I want to find constructive ways to exist with this world. I still get angry when I think about the injustice that exists in the world. My anger may even be misplaced and misguided at times.

Anger toward the Khmer Rouge is valid, but many people carry misplaced anger. I have heard people questioning the integrity of someone wearing *kromma*, a traditional scarf used mainly by farmers. The sight of *kromma* may have triggered memories of the Killing Fields, but to think that people wearing *kromma* are Khmer Rouge sympathizers is ignorant. *Kromma* have been used for generations by Cambodian farmers. *Kromma* should not be seen as a symbol of the Khmer Rouge, even though they used it as a part of their clothing. The healing of Cambodia and Cambodians include understanding and distinguishing the Khmer Rouge from the Khmer population and harmless practices that were an integral part of life in Cambodia prior to and apart from the Killing Fields.

There are those who associate the word p*ok* (father) and *mae* (mother) with the Khmer Rouge. The Khmer Rouge was pushing for an agrarian society, extolling many things related to farmers and farming. They evacuated everyone to the countryside and forced all people to address their parents with the same terms used by farmers. The words we use to address our parents convey what part of the country we came from and our family's socioeconomic status. This can be seen in the English language with the formal *mother* and *father* as compared to the every day *mom* and *dad* to the more colloquial *pop*, *pa*, and *ma*. *Pok* and *mae* are used by the sons and daughters of farmers and *pa* and *mak* are used by the sons and daughters of urbanites. Not many people seem willing to learn and acknowledge the different regional terms that can be used to address our parents, and to accept that no one term is better than another.

Searching for Inspiration

I have searched for inspiration in words and stories that describe the survival of humanity in the Khmer spirit. These included autobiographies on the Killing Fields and different creative productions on Cambodia ranging from books to music to films. Within these creative productions and inspirational works, I see the strengths of the Cambodian people. The films of Rithy Panh, the music of Prach, and films like the *Refugee, The Flute Player,* and even Angelina Jolie's passion for Cambodia are part of my collection of inspiration. These inspirations are the stories of my country and people; they are created by Khmer people or written about Khmer people, our plight and survival.

I have read autobiographies that describe the Khmer Rouge regime, and among these, *When Broken Glass Floats* by Chanrithy Him is my favorite. This book underlines a search for magic on a trek to the Himalayas, reminding me of what it means to be Khmer, and unearthing Khmer beliefs, sayings, and superstitions that were buried within my psyche. Written with a great deal of sensitivity and insight, *When Broken Glass Floats* also scrutinizes the complexity of the civil war and human nature.

When Broken Glass Floats is the author's journey to find the magic of a world lost as a result of the Khmer Rouge. This book, as a personal account of the Khmer Rouge regime, is also my personal journey as a reader and a Khmer person. Through this magical journey, my own forgotten memories are awakened and many traditional beliefs that I have pushed to the back of my mind resurface.

Each chapter begins with poignant sayings and quotes from newspaper articles that give insights into the political situation in Cambodia, while footnotes explain different Cambodian proverbs, practices, and beliefs. Under the Khmer Rouge, new rules came into existence, conflicting with and undermining many existing beliefs and values. Him tells us that "the Khmer Rouge wish to rule not only our inner spiritual lives but our outward appearance as well. They require girls and women to wear their hair short. The rule is a deliberate slap in the face of our culture, which prizes the traditional beauty of long hair" (p. 99).

Him connects the foreshadowing of the war in Cambodia with a Khmer superstition which states, "when the tail of the comet pointed to a particular place, Cambodia would be drawn into war with that country" (p. 31). Him also discusses the terms of endearment that Khmer people use to address their spouses and children, words like *pa vear*, which is explained as "The familiar address of a wife to her husband, a term of endearment" (father of the children) (p. 196).

I was too young to have memories of the Killing Fields, but I have heard enough stories to feel connected to it. There were gaps missing in my memory and this book filled those gaps. *When Broken Glass Floats* is poetic and touching, a book rooted in the author's desire to let the world know about the tragic death of her family. It begins when her memories are awakened as a result of her work as an interpreter and interviewer for the Khmer Adolescent Project, studying post-traumatic stress disorder among Cambodian survivors. This is a story of triumph, survival, and hope written from the Khmer soul of a Cambodian-American woman.

When Broken Glass Floats is a book with two moving and powerful purposes: one, as a therapeutic tool for the author, and, two, as a reminder of an event that should never have occurred. The author describes her book as a way "to use the power of words to caution the world, and in the process to heal myself" (p. 23). The process of writing the book became a trek to the Himalayas, "a search to recapture the long-lost magic in [her] life" (p. 23). My travels have taken me to the Himalayas. I have been seeking magic for my own healing like the author of *When Broken Glass Floats*. The process of reading her book and other autobiographies has provided much healing. I recommend this book for everyone who is interested in this subject, but in particular to Cambodian-Americans, because this book can take you on a journey into yourself, your soul, memories, and past.

Recognizing Inaccurate Stories

My journey has been filled with inspiration and disappointment. Ignorance and misplaced anger are plentiful when it comes to the Killing Fields. People want to blame someone else, as indicated in "Drunken Conversations." They try to disassociate themselves, their backgrounds, and their families from the Killing Fields at all cost. The way we interpret the war depends on our respective background. The children of rich Cambodians have a tendency to blame the peasants for their ignorance and superstitions; the children of peasants have a tendency to blame the rich for their corruption and exploitation. Both groups, the rich and the poor, the farmers and the city dwellers, are at fault; corruption, exploitation, and blind love of the monarchy all led to the rise and victory of the Khmer Rouge.

I have also tried to distance myself from the Khmer Rouge, finding solace in the fact that my parents were civilians throughout the war. They were neither the heroes of the Lon Nol Army nor the monsters of the Khmer Rouge Army. The Lon Nol Army has been seen as heroic by some and as the destroyer of Cambodia by others. There are stories of high-ranking officials in the Lon Nol Army creating lists of phantom soldiers and pocketing their salaries. On paper, they would send two hundred men to fight, while in reality, they sent only one hundred.

I have found healing and inspiration within different autobiographies that describe life in the Killing Fields, but I have also encountered disappointment. Loung Ung's *First They Killed My Father* was a national bestseller that came out in 2000, but it is a book that should be read with caution. The author is too young to have reliable memories and does not possess the insight of an enlightened adult. The book is riddled with carelessness: unreliable memories and inaccurate information. When *First They Killed My Father* came out, it generated a rampage of discussion among different Internet newsgroups and forums concerning the misinformation in the book. For instance, Ung wrote about a family trip to Angkor Wat, which took place in 1973 or 1974 when she "was only three or four years old" (p. 109). I had a discussion with a former Lon Nol soldier who was in Siem Reap at that time and he was adamant that Angkor Wat was not accessible because the Khmer Rouge was in full control of the area.

Cambodia had been fighting a civil war since 1970, so it is hard to believe that there were people vacationing at that time, especially in a region that was controlled by the Khmer Rouge. But the book contains a picture of the family trip to "Angkor Wat," which was taken at Wat Phnom, a temple in Phnom Penh.

Controversy continues to surround the book and the author. For instance, an article in the *Boston Globe*, "Revisiting a Painful Chapter in Cambodia" (April 2001), states:

> Loung Ung also said she was afraid. She had received death threats and hate mail, she said, mostly from fellow Cambodian-Americans. Some attacked her for being half-Chinese while writing on behalf of Cambodians; some continue to deny

the genocide's existence. Loung Ung worried the attacks would multiply if the book were translated into Khmer.

I have never met a Cambodian-American who claimed that the Killing Fields did not happen. I can not help but wonder if Ung misunderstood the letters she received. Instead of denying the existence of the Killing Fields, maybe they were merely denying that the Killing Fields were a form of "ethnic cleansing" and questioning incidents like the trip to Angkor Wat.

As I read the article, I wondered why Ung would receive threatening letters when there were many autobiographies prior to hers and no other authors had been threatened. Many of the previous authors were Cambodian of Chinese descent and they were not threatened. The author of *When Broken Glass Floats* is also Chinese-Cambodian and she was not attacked for writing on behalf of Cambodians. The difference may have been the inaccuracies in the book.

Exaggerated stories of surviving atrocities are not unknown. It even exists within the Jewish community; for example, the story of Deli Strummer, which has been written in the Washington Post. The Jewish community also has a website that debunks exaggerated stories of surviving the Holocaust. I hope the Cambodian community will reach a point where our need for heroes will not surpass our need to recognize and challenge inaccurate stories that misrepresents Cambodia's tragedy. We should want the world to read books that are poignant like Anne Frank's Diary versus sensationalized story like Deli Strummer.

Ethnic Cleansing

When applied to the Killing Fields, the term *ethnic cleansing* is misused. The Killing Fields were a genocidal campaign to eradicate class within Cambodian society. The people who were hurt the most were members of the rich, upper class.

I have seen Internet discussions where people refuse to accept the idea of Khmer killing Khmer. They argue that the Khmer Rouge regime was a tool of the Viet Cong. This may have been true in the beginning when members of the Khmer Rouge were being trained by the Viet Cong, but once they controlled Cambodia, it was their policies and actions that caused two million deaths. The Killing Fields were Khmer killing Khmer.

There have been many fascinating and educational discussions about the term *ethnic cleansing* as it relates to the Killing Fields. One person offered the explanation that Chinese-Cambodians in his part of Cambodia were persecuted more severely than the rest; thus, he ventured to say that the term *ethnic cleansing* is appropriate. I dared to ask if the persecution was solely based on the fact that they were Chinese-Cambodians or if it was also because they were from the city, a group that the Khmer Rouge viewed as corrupt; hence their persecution had nothing to do with their ethnicity and everything to do with their socioeconomic background.

The killing committed by the Khmer Rouge regime was far from ethnic cleansing. Many of the Khmer Rouge leaders were light-skinned individuals who were Chinese-Cambodian themselves. The Killing Fields were a genocide of Khmer killing Khmer, and some Khmer are of Chinese descent but they are still Khmer.

The Word Yuon

The word *Yuon*, like the term *ethnic cleansing*, has been a topic of many discussions in my journey. *Yuon* is a Khmer word that means Vietnamese. It is neither derogatory nor flattering. When my parents became friends with our Vietnamese-Cambodian neighbors, we called them *Yuon*. As we call Cambodia, *Srok Khmer*, we also called Vietnam *Srok Yuon*, land of the *Yuon*.

In "Khmer Language and the Term Yuon," Bora Touch argues:

> To say that "yuon" means "savages," critics of the term are likely reliant on the Khmer Rouge's definition from KR Black Book (1978) p.9, a definition that is incorrect and baseless and was included by the KR for the purpose of propaganda. Some Khmer, including Khmer Krom, believe that "yuon" actually derives from "Yuonan," the Chinese word for Vietnam. Others believe it comes from the Yaun (Khan) dynasty, against whose armies both the Khmer and Cham did battle.

But in Cambodia, *Yuon* has somehow become a politically incorrect word that some view as derogatory.

Many Cambodian-Americans and local Cambodians disagree on the meaning of the word *Yuon*. If I were to accept that the meaning changed due to some occurrence in Cambodia and that people outside of Cambodia were out of the loop, I would hope that the world could accept that *Yuon* can still be used neutrally without a supposedly derogatory connotation. But I'm not convinced that the word has changed in meaning. I think people may change it for their own agenda. Unfortunately, it can bring misunderstanding and animosity when *Yuon* is used in Cambodia.

The new acceptable term for *Yuon* is *Vietnam*. As pronounced by Khmer people with our unique accent, it sounds like "Yak-nam," "Yak" being the mystical giant that eats humans. I prefer to think of my Vietnamese friends as *Yuon* rather than as blood-thirsty giants.

I also saw an Internet discussion asserting that the Laotian word for *Vietnamese* is *Yuon* or *Kaew*. To be able to live and have the dignity to use your language without others telling you that certain words have a negative connotation is a luxury that Cambodians do not have.

Vindicating Gods

My journey to come to terms with the Killing Fields began as a spiritual dilemma, long before reading different autobiographies and engaging in discussion and debate. It began when I learned about the world and what people had suffered in the Killing Fields and the Holocaust.

I grew up believing in the sacredness of the world. My parents, like most Cambodians, are Buddhists. Their religious practice combines Buddhism, with its concepts of karma and reincarnation, with animism, spirit beings that reside in nature. They are devoted Buddhists, even to this day. Although a church group in New Mexico sponsored my family's journey to America, after a few months in New Mexico, we moved to California in search of a Cambodian community and Buddhist temples.

My parents embedded my religious upbringing with spirits and magic, life after death, and reincarnation, but they also asserted that *preah ker preah*, in other words, God is God, whether people called him God, Buddha, Mohammad, or Jesus. I was quite fortunate to have open-minded parents who taught me to appreciate the differences in the world and it has continued to be part of my own value in appreciating diversity that ranges from ethnicity to culture, religion and sexual orientation.

My parents sent me to church when I was younger, which was typical of many Cambodian families who were sponsored by church groups. My mother also had a practical reason: the interaction would allow me to learn English faster. My mother felt that a place of religion could only teach me to be a good and loving person. Unfortunately, it was not true. Even at a young age, I saw something in the church that was harmful. My mother sent me to church with good faith that it could only teach me to be a better person, but the church was teaching intolerance. The church labeled other religions as "false"; many people came to my house to convert my parents. I stopped going to church and my mother did not argue after her firsthand experience of being told she would go to hell unless she relinquishes her religious practices.

I respect most religions and their goals, but traditional practices hold a greater appeal for me. I feel a religious reverence in most places of worship but Buddhist temples represent my culture and upbringing. Native American beliefs resonate with my soul, reflecting my Khmer upbringing. There is a correlation between the Khmer belief in the loss of a soul during a traumatic experience (*lous proloeung*) and the concept of calling the soul back, or soul retrieval as practiced by shamanism. I also revere Wicca, a practice that values the sacred goddess and feminine power. I am a person who agrees with the New Age concept that my moral values are between me and God alone.

When I saw the movie *The Killing Fields*, I was too young to understand the complexities of the story but I remembered my parents saying, "That is why we left

Cambodia." A few years later, when I was in high school, I saw documentaries about the Holocaust with images of the death camps and half-dead, starving bodies flashing across the T.V. screen; my belief in God shattered. The power of God was no longer beautiful and sacred in my eyes. God should have not allowed the Killing Fields and the Holocaust to occur.

For a period of a year, sporadically, I had a recurring dream in which I was killed in a rice field. I saw myself as an old woman dressed in black, digging ditches and being killed in the field because the Khmer Rouge were unhappy with my work. In order to maintain my sanity, I pushed the nightmares, God, and the cruelty of humanity into the back of my mind. I had many volatile conversations with God at the top of my silent screams.

After five years of ignoring God and the belief in a Higher Being, I finally considered the possibility that the purpose of our existence is above and beyond pain and suffering. It was the openness of different New Age concepts that helped me with my transition and introduced the idea of the interconnectedness of the Universe and the notion that each one of us came to earth to learn a lesson (or lessons). Some of us have more to learn, unleashing a lot of pain and suffering on earth.

After a great deal of soul searching and exploring different practices and beliefs, I have finally allowed myself to believe in the sacredness of the Universe again. I still do not understand everything about the Universe, the evolution of human life, the beauty and cruelty of humanity, but I believe in the Universe and the strength of the human soul and in life after death. The epiphany of my spiritual faith is not enough to forgive Hitler or Pol Pot, but I am no longer preoccupied with the hope that they are burning in Hell.

I still continue to learn from and to evaluate my passion, anger, and sympathy for the world. I am human. I still get overwhelmed by depression, greed, desire, unrealistic expectations, and anger. At the same time, I can also forgive, forget, and move on. But these are lessons that are a part of my journey and growth. Maybe, I have finally understood the Scheme of the Universe: There is no God to vindicate. The stardust is merely a power that gives us life and consciousness and exemplifies the possibility that all of us are responsible for the kind of world we create by choosing love over hate and forgiveness over revenge.

PART FIVE

Musings of a Traveler

The Nature of Nomads

Nomads move to the rhythm of the Earth's rotation. I am a nomad that has been swept around the world as a refugee and a traveler.

In my travels, I have seen beauty and cruelty. I noticed that Earth is adorned with life-nourishing fruits and radiant jewels. Mother Earth is painted with flowing rivers, running creeks, and singing trees. Her jungles are occupied by wild and untamed animals. She is natural and beautiful, soft and feminine, a Mother to people, animals, and trees. She has been domesticated with cities and villages. She is a Woman with many years to Her name. Although the years of Her life have not diminished Her beauty, like an aging woman, She suffers the wrinkle of time. She has known joys and violence ripping across Her body.

I have met many people on Earth and learned about different cultures in different lands. I have been forced to journey around the world in search of asylum because of my country's atrocities. I have also been endowed with an innate desire to travel the world in search of adventure and the meaning of life.

I have many more lands to explore, but this is a lifelong goal so every corner shall be surveyed before the end of my days.

I have traveled far and wide, embarking on an inner journey to cope with the beauty and the cruelty of life. In my reflections, I want to share stories of my travels, stories of beauty, and stories of a journey into the history of human cruelty.

Cambodia: The Journey Home

Although my trip to Cambodia was not the first time I traveled outside of America, it was the first trip in which I truly journeyed inside myself. In October of 1998, I traveled to Cambodia for three months after securing an internship through a Cambodian family that I met in Thailand.

My mother did not want me to go because a month earlier, a demonstration against Hun Sen ended in shooting. Her concern was valid, but I was too close to Cambodia to let the opportunity slip away. The year prior to my trip, I had felt a burning desire to visit *Srok Khmer*, the land of my people, my past, and ancestors.

I had three phone conversations with my mother. She was adamant that I should not go. I assured her that I would not go unless it was safe. During the third conversation, I was already in *Srok Khmer*, and she was in no position to dispute my decision.

I read *Off the Rail of Phnom Penh: Girls, Guns, and Ganja* before the trip, a book that conveys disturbing tales of sexual escapades, drug use, and the exploitation of a country weakened by war and moral dilapidation. Cambodia was a sanctuary for debauchery as she attempted to recover from years of war. Young girls become prostitutes and were objectified with careless disregard. I was distraught and disturbed about the situation in Cambodia.

I arrived in Cambodia feeling nervous and excited. My heart shattered as the memories of my homeland came alive with the sight of scattered palm trees dotting across the empty fields. I was returning home, returning to a place of sadness, a place where survival is the mode of life and happiness is a luxury many people cannot afford.

I walked out of the airport expecting someone to be waiting, but no one was there. I was accosted from all sides by taxi drivers vying for fares. Fortunately, I had the address and directions to the office where I was to begin my internship. The taxi driver asked if I was Filipino. I told him I was Khmer but he refused to believe me, even though we were speaking Khmer to each other.

Throughout my stay in Cambodia, I had problems convincing people that I was Khmer. I have always considered myself to be fairly fluent in Khmer, and I have Khmer features, but the way I talked, walked, and carried myself must have indicated that I was a foreigner. Everyone in Thailand insisted I was Thai, but everyone in Cambodia insisted that I was anything but Cambodian.

When I explained to my taxi driver that I am Khmer living abroad, he proposed marriage, telling me about his life as an orphan, trying to elicit sympathy, and encouraging me to take him to the United States and a better life. Needless to say, I was happy to be free of his company.

Four months in Thailand did not prepare me for Cambodia. I had thought Thailand was chaotic and dirty, but Cambodia was worse. When I arrived at my new home, two guards and a maid admitted to knowing I would arrive, but said they did not know when it would be. I chose a room to settle in and fell into bed feeling relieved.

The internship was informal with minimal work. I was reviewing literature for a conference on the meaning of community in Cambodia. Unfortunately, I did not complete the project because I contracted typhoid during the last few weeks from contaminated food since I ate everything in sight. But during my three months in Cambodia, I socialized and explored. Gradually, I made new friends, both local Khmers and Cambodian-Americans who had returned to work in Cambodia; some had been there for three years, others had been there for five.

During my stay, I participated in a variety of leisure

activities including fishing in a rented hut along the river, a new and interesting concept.

I was living and participating in the normal activities of life in Cambodia. Every morning, I strolled to the market to buy fresh vegetables and meat. I washed my own clothes by hand, and the stains never came out, no matter how hard I scrubbed. I also kept busy by introducing myself to a student organization near the house and made a deal with one of the members. Every day, I spent an hour teaching him English and he spent an hour teaching me Khmer, to improve my reading skills. I also became friends with one of the other teachers there who asked me to speak to his students with my "American accent." The first question his students asked was "Do you have a sweetheart in the U.S?" After I answered no, the second question was "Are you my teacher's sweetheart?" I was embarrassed and pleasantly surprised at the use of the word *sweetheart* instead of *boyfriend.*

I possess in my memory a pleasant trip to Kep on a moonlit night, with stars, swaying palm leaves, and a gentle wind that caressed softly. I leaned against a bending palm and looked toward the sky, engulfed by the romance of the night and stars. I inhaled the night air into my lungs and smiled, knowing that I was standing on my motherland. I also met children who were amused by my catching pond skaters, little bugs with long slender legs that glide across the water like skiers. I had never seen them before and found them fascinating. As I tried to scoop them into my hands, a few children observed me with curiosity. They looked at each other and asked, "Why is the aunty trying to catch 'water fleas?'" "Water fleas" is the literal translation of the Cambodian name for these bugs. I had never seen "water fleas" before but now that I knew what they were, I stood, straightened myself up, and walked away feeling a little embarrassed and amused.

Halfway through my stay, my classmate and friend, Taylor, came to visit, and we traveled to Angkor Wat together. Traveling with a white man in Cambodia was an interesting experience. When we arrived in Siem Reap, we were given a room with one bed and I asked for a room with two beds, which confused the proprietor of the guesthouse because we are either together or we are not. We should have shared one bed or stayed in two separate rooms.

The children at Angkor Wat came up to Taylor and asked, "Is she your *husband?*" There were many kids chasing after us, offering their products or service as tour guides.

Angkor is a place of dreams and fantasies, a fairy-tale city of long ago, and I had the privilege to visit it, but I was more than merely a visitor. I was a daughter, an heir to the lifeblood, of that great city. I wished my family and friends could have been with me to share the beauty of that experience.

Angkor Wat and Banteay Srey are two of my favorite temples along with Bayon and Ta Prohm. During my exploration of Angkor Wat, Taylor and I were caught in a thunderstorm. We ran for shelter under one of the structures on the compound, sitting there with monks and vendors waiting for the rain to stop. It was strangely uplifting to come together for protection from the rain and I felt strangely honored to share those moments with my countrymen.

I was also fortunate to observe the water festival during my trip. I had heard stories from my mother about the excited crowds and festive mood, but her stories were more exciting than the actual event. I could see why someone like my mother, a person from a small village, would remember it as a grand event, and so it was for her.

Toward the end of my trip, I went to visit my mother's siblings, my aunts and uncles, and their children, my cousins, in my hometown of Battambang province. This was a meeting of strangers, but I saw the family resemblance immediately. My mother's facial features and beauty were echoed in the faces of my aunts and cousins. I went to my mother's village and caught a glimpse of her life there, living without a bathroom or running water, digging holes and using bushes as lavatories. I walked around the rice field and garden, meeting trees, bushes, and shrubs that my mother had grown and tended.

The road was dusty and I was dirty and sweaty most of the time. I rode an old bicycle on the road with my younger cousin and I could imagine the fear my mother felt during those last few days before my birth.

I took pictures of my relatives under the mango tree that my mother grew and tended; it was a foot in height when she left Cambodia, and twenty years later, it towered over my family members, feeding them over many seasons.

During the trip to Battambang, I was having night fevers, but I refused to go to the hospital since I had so little time with them.

When I returned to Phnom Penh, I was diagnosed with typhoid. It was two weeks before my return to America and I had to be hospitalized for a week. The doctors were concerned about a secondary infection in my appendix. I was afraid I might die if the doctor operated on me, having heard horror stories about the hospitals in Cambodia. Facing the possibility that I might die in the operating room, I realized that I may be Khmer at heart, but California is my home. My family and friends and many things that I love are in California. I knew then that although I hoped to return to Cambodia again and again in my lifetime and may even live or work there for periods of time, California is home and I will always return to it.

When I left Cambodia, I was too numb and exhausted

from my recovery to feel the sadness of leaving or the joy of coming home to my family and friends.

When I look back and remember my favorite sights and feelings in Cambodia, an image that embodies friendship and love lingers in my mind. In every village I would see two little children, either two little boys or two little girls, walking along the dusty road, half covered in dirt, wearing rags, and holding hands. Even though life in Cambodia is difficult, her children have someone to hold their hands to make the world less forbidding. These were the images and feelings that I would look for on my next visit and on many more visits after that.

Cambodia: A Whirlwind Tour

My second trip to Cambodia was a two-week whirlwind tour from December 1999 through January 2000.

I met up with a friend from the U.S. who was visiting Cambodia with his mother and sister. I stayed with them and their relatives in Phnom Penh. We went to Angkor Wat to celebrate the ending of the second millennium. I fulfilled my wish to see Angkor with friends, but we were rushing to see everything and did not make time to savor the moment. However, I did visit Phnom Kulen and the reservoir, two places that I did not visit during my first trip.

At midnight on January 1, 2000, I stood on the balcony of the hotel and watched the firework displays welcoming the New Year. I was alone because everyone was too exhausted to stay up until midnight. The fireworks glittered over Angkor like precious jewels in brilliant colors.

I also met with old friends from my first trip and visited the places I used to haunt. I noticed many improvements in Cambodia. The streets in front of the palace were cleaner and there was grass along the sidewalks. There were no taxi drivers at the airport pulling at you and your luggage for fares or hagglers shoving magazines into your face.

I crossed the Japanese Bridge many times to hang out at my favorite place, swinging in a hammock eating balut eggs, corn, and papaya salad.

The trip was aptly called a "whirlwind tour." The trip offered no time to feel or to closely scrutinize my feelings. I came, saw, and left.

I saw, felt, smelled, and tasted the essence and color of Cambodia, teasing my senses before returning to America.

Cambodia: Perception and Deception

From December 26, 2004 to Janury 14, 2005, I returned to Cambodia for a third time. I went with two people whose company I have always enjoyed. The trip was great all around. I saw my relatives again. I went to Cambodia to be with friends, to see old friends, and make new ones. I accomplished all of that flawlessly, but more importantly, I know I never need a reason to visit Cambodia.

I perceived it to be a good trip. My perception was true, but it was also deceptive. The first night back home, I could not sleep. I could attribute it to jet lag or to the mild insomnia I developed during my trip, but the truth was I did not want to sleep. My mind was running here and there and my emotions were in turmoil. It was the aftershock of Cambodia. Perhaps the most important reflections were those formulated after the trip, and not what I thought about, felt, or tried to project while I was in Cambodia.

I felt a little broken on my return and I reflected on Cambodia and my travels.

The first time I went to Cambodia, I was following an inner desire to see the country of my birth. The second trip was the result of temptation and proximity as I was studying in India. I went on a third trip at the request of a friend, but it too became my own quest, with new situations to evaluate and consider.

We saw and did more than we thought was possible. We laughed and smiled. We ate until we were full; we ate until we had stomachaches, but we continued to gorge on our favorite fruits. We were frustrated and flustered, uncomfortable and dirty most of the time, but I loved the sense of adventure that Cambodia provided.

I saw my relatives in Battambang. They were wearisome at times but they also had the power to expose my emotions, leaving me raw and empty. I ignored the sadness in my heart when I left my mother's village even though my aunt asked me to stay for a few more hours. I left because I could not face all the emotions that I felt nor scrutinize the feeling of helplessness that their poverty induced. I left to visit other parts of Cambodia, places that could not touch my soul the way my relatives can.

The journey ended as it always does and I came back home. The plane landed at 6:30 p.m. in LAX, and I arrived home two hours later. After I ate, I remembered that a long, hot shower was necessary after the many hours on the plane and the feeling of never being clean while I was in Cambodia. I enjoyed every moment of my hot shower, feeling extremely refreshed. I snuggled under my blanket, trying to find the comfort of home and the sense of familiarity, but my mind drifted. Cambodia makes my heart ache, but I have a love affair with her that I cannot end. It was a trip of indulgences. Our friends in Cambodia, old and new, spoiled us and I loved every moment of it.

I did not make time to go to clubs or karaoke bars even though I wanted to visit them again. After the days' outings, I was too exhausted. The truth was, a part of me was afraid to go. I am definitely less brave and less curious on this trip or maybe I am afraid to revisit what I felt when I read *Off the Rail of Phnom Penh: Girls, Guns, and Ganja.* I want to understand that world but I was afraid to touch it. The bits and pieces that I knew were already overwhelming. However, prior to the trip, I read *Memoirs of a Geisha.* I wanted to read a geisha story as it related to the karaoke girls in Cambodia...

I returned to the U.S. with many souvenirs from Cambodia: emotions, thoughts, and ideas. One of my favorite pairs of jeans was plastered with the red dirt of Cambodia and it has not washed off completely even though I have laundered it many times.

The adjustment period left me bewildered and confused, mistaking sleep deprivation for hunger, but a week later, the effect of Cambodia was almost erased and it became another trip with more memories. I perceived it to be a good trip, and maybe that perception is not deceptive, even if at times I had felt pain and heartache.

During my visit, I scanned the country for images of "true friendship and love that carry us through life" and I found it throughout Cambodia, scattered in great quantity, like the palm trees.

Cambodia: Revisiting the Same Question

I was in Cambodia from December 2005 to January 2006, the same time of year as my previous trip, but I stayed a week longer. During this trip, the questions that I was asked were "Do you like Cambodia? Will you come back to live here?"

I think I have discussed this already in many different ways and reflections. But here we go again; there are things about Cambodia that I like and things that I dislike and despise.

To be honest, I do NOT like Cambodia, dusty, dirty, and pushy. Why do I keep going back then? Because I LOVE Cambodia... Maybe I have been brainwashed to feel the connection that I do for her, like a member of the family. You do not like her but you have to love her. Maybe you don't have to love her but you do anyway. I love her despite all the things I hate about her, the things that frustrate and hurt.

The trips to Cambodia are always good, no matter how terrible they are. To be with someone you love is always good. To feel and wish that the one you love should have more, should be better, is always bittersweet. It is always good. It is always bittersweet.

I love the comfort of my home in California, so do I want to live in Cambodia? Not really... I do not have to be on her soil to love her and want the best for her. I have yet to cut the umbilical cord connecting me to Cambodia and I do not think I ever will; but I am a creature of comfort, physically and emotionally. Cambodia is not comfortable.

My mantra for Cambodia is "I'm brave and strong!" It is my mantra for life but I need it even more in Cambodia. I remember it before I walk outside to catch a *motodop*; before I go into the bathroom to take a cold shower, I chant it.

Maybe I need to live in an air-conditioned mansion and have a driver and a maid to make it in Cambodia. Maybe I need to change some of my ideas and fears of what it might mean to become accustomed to the sights and sorrows of Cambodia.

Touring the World

England: July 1996

My travels have revealed that magic, beauty, and romance exist on Earth, but are hidden to those who refuse to open their mind to it. I travel to see the dance and rhythm of different people. The world is decorated by ancient cultures with temples and ruins of temples built by people to worship their makers. I travel to see the remnant of this romantic world.

Twelve years after I set foot in America, in July 1996, I took my first trip abroad. I went to England to study Shakespeare and walk in the footsteps of my heroes and heroines, both fictitious and real. Life during my travels seemed special, even the trees and rivers were somehow exceptional.

Hamlet may have asked himself "To be or not to be?" but I asked myself, "To travel or not to travel?" and the answer is always irrefutably yes.

During my trip, I took a pilgrimage to Canterbury to listen to the whispers of the fictitious characters in Chaucer's *The Canterbury Tales* and to remember their struggles and reasons for pilgrimage.

Besides chasing literary characters, I also pursued historical sites—visiting Warwick and Edinburgh castles on a weekend trip to Scotland, catching an eight-hour night bus, getting there and trying to see and do as much as possible, and returning to Stratford in time for the Monday morning lecture.

I had an epiphany during my trip to England: I am American. I defended America when people criticize it, especially because these criticisms were based on faulty assumptions. The trip abroad helped me to decipher a part of my identity and finally accept that I was not merely Cambodian. I am Cambodian-American.

Thailand: June to October 1998

After England, I visited Thailand, a place close to Cambodia, spurring memories of childhood and life in the refugee camps. I went to Thailand through a study abroad program. After fourteen years in America, my life in Southeast Asia had become distant memories, so when I returned to Thailand, I experienced culture shock from what I perceived to be a strange, dirty country.

Even though, I chose Thailand largely as a stepping-stone to Cambodia, it has become one of my favorite vacation spots. I love the spicy, sour taste of Thailand and the tropical fruits of Southeast Asia. I still have a vivid memory of sitting on the wall of a temple watching an electric storm flashing into the night, illuminating the structures of the villages across the valley.

I found Thai people to be friendly, easygoing, helpful, and genuine (for the most part). Before I went to Thailand, I was warned by many Cambodians to keep my identity a secret or suffer being insulted. Everyone in Thailand kept insisting that I was Thai, excusing my inability to speak Thai as my upbringing in America. I was amused and touched that they think I am one of theirs. When I admitted that I am Cambodian, they still insisted that "my face looks Thai."

In the morning, I rode an old bicycle to Chiang Mai University, chased by the neighborhood dogs, braving traffic and praying for safety. My host family attempted to speak English to me the first week I lived with them, but they spoke Thai to me as if I was fluent the following week. Our conversation was limited as I nodded in agreement, pretending that I understand. When my time with the host family ended, I moved into an apartment with two vegetarian roommates who failed to convert me.

Taylor was an insightful friend who thinks I have an antenna for detecting and finding Cambodians and it was true. I met a Cambodian family living in Chiang Mai and a Cambodian-American who was working for the U.S. consulate.

During our nine-day trip to see the former capital and historical sites, including the Khmer temple of Phnom Rung, I met Cambodians living in Thailand who spoke Khmer with a strong Thai accent.

India: June to December 1999

India is the country that ruins me for everything and prepares me for anything. Nothing can be as beautiful or as frustrating as my experiences in India (except for Cambodia, but Cambodia is personal).

I spent six months studying and traveling in India from June to December of 1999. India was a challenge in every way possible: poverty, beggars, pollution, sanitation problems, overly aggressive people, staring, and sexual harassment. There were moment when I rose to these challenges, but for the most part, I submitted to my anger and frustration, screaming at people to leave me alone.

I survived six months of India, especially Delhi, a place that even locals consider the worst city in India. I am pleased with the experiences, the excitement, and the adventure, but I wish I had behaved with more grace. It was a wonderful trip because I saw beauty in people's smiles, culture, temples, and art despite everything.

My classmates and I spent the first month in Missouri, a station at the foothills of the Himalayas, studying Hindi. On the way to Missouri, I was in a car with a crazy driver who zigzagged up the mountain on a small, windy road honking furiously at the cars ahead. I was not surprised when we hit the car in front but I was surprised I made it in one piece. The weather in Missouri, like the driver, was unpredictable—cold, wet, and rainy, sunny, clear, and foggy, but the land was permeated with beautiful, mildewed trees.

In the foothills of the Himalayas, I recalled the Khmer legends of my childhood about wise old men living in *Phnom Hamapean*. I did not meet these wise hermits, but I met female herders during my solitude walks. For the first time I regretted not learning enough Hindi to communicate, but we still connected as I counted from one to thirty-one for them and they showed their appreciation with sweet laughter.

From Missouri, we journeyed to another magical place, Yamunotri, the source of the Yamuna River, the second most sacred river in India. At the temple, people bathed in the river and the hot springs to cleanse their sins. We also visited an ancient village that some consider to be the first village in India.

In Missouri, I met a Cambodian woman, Saron, who was married to an American named Danny and their daughter, Leeta.

After the month passed, we said good-bye to friends in Missouri and returned to Delhi, the real India: chaotic, dirty, and polluted. In Delhi, there were cows roaming the neighborhood eating trash and producing cow dung everywhere. In some areas, the stench of human feces was overwhelming. The heat was sweltering and the moment there was an electric outage and the fan stopped, I woke up from my deep sleep. The children of rich Indians and ambassadors could not believe that Americans students would choose to stay in Kingsway Cemp, Old Delhi.

My roommates and I were fully initiated to India by a

pervert who masturbated in front of us. Despite this set-
back, my roommates and I had memorable adventures in
India. We rented bicycles in Sanchi, visited Buddhist stu-
pas and explored the Udaigiri Caves in the rain.

I met students from Cambodia studying in Delhi. After
I met my Cambodian friend from the international hostel,
he took me to New Delhi to meet other Cambodians who
were living in a Khmer temple there. Dressed in sari, even
the Cambodian boys thought I was Indian.

India celebrates many religious holidays. I went to
Mathura and Vrindavan to celebrate Krishna's birthday.
Early in the morning, people went to the temple and wor-
shipped for three hours with song and dance. The Hindu
monks chanted, sang, and danced in front of the shrine
while worshippers danced and clapped in the layman seat-
ing. The music started out slowly and increased in tempo.
People swayed their bodies to the music and then danced
in a trancelike frenzy. I was caught up in the festive mood,
clapping along with everyone, dancing, and pushing my
way to the altar to be splashed by the holy water.

The most meaningful religious visit for me was a trip
to Bodhgaya to see the bo tree where Buddha gained his
enlightenment. The trip connected me to my religious and
cultural upbringing in the Buddhist tradition. I felt hum-
bled and honored to be at the site.

In Varanasi, the most sacred place for Hindus, I was
overwhelmed by fury and resentment. I hated the smell
of feces and cow dung. Men stared with lecherous eyes
while women seemed to blame us for the harassment we
received. I glared at beggars, young, old, or crippled and
hawkers trying to get my attention. I also saw some of the
most disgusting, pitiful, and traumatizing sights there—
people with leprosy in bandages, moaning pitifully. I saw
a struggling goat being sacrificed. I was emotionally ex-

hausted. I hated India then. I lost my temper at a rickshaw driver. I was in Varanasi during a large Hindu celebration and it seemed like everybody in India was there, pushing and stepping on me.

In the congested traffic of Varanasi, my rickshaw was hit by an impatient driver. As I fell off, I saw myself falling in slow motion, landing hard on the ground. Onlookers helped me with my bruises and cuts by rubbing gasoline onto my skin, a method that Cambodian refugees employed in the camps.

After Varanasi, I visited Khajuraho, a small, quiet little town with beautiful temples. It was peaceful and relaxing and I was in a better mood. Khajuraho is famous for its erotic sculptures so there were hawkers selling keys chain of copulating couples. The bus ride to and from Khajuraho was beyond discomfort. People packed into the aisle and climbed out of the windows to get out, stepping on us many times.

However, a trip to the Golden Temple, which means "Pool of Nectar" in Amritsar, was pleasant. The temple is the holiest shrine of the Sikh religion. The Sikhs are known for their kindness and honesty. I enjoyed the day at Amritsar and their hospitality. We had to cover our heads once we entered the temple and shoes were not allowed inside, not even if you tried to hide them in your backpack.

I also traveled to other parts of India, visiting the rock-cut caves of Ajanta and Ellora before continuing to Bangalore, Hampi, Goa, and Bombay. Hampi was magical and beautiful. Many people tried to guess my nationality and I said I was from the Northeast of India.

After Hampi, we went to Jog Fall, the highest waterfall in India and hung out at the beaches of Goa. Then we were off to Bombay, where we stayed with the family of a friend and I bought a ticket for the museum by paying five rupees instead of one hundred and fifty, which was the price for foreigners.

During my time in India, I was miserable and angry, but at the same time I felt inspired and uplifted. I saw the influence of India on Cambodia.

Nepal: December 1999

Nepal was a much-needed vacation from India. People in Nepal seemed friendly and gracious, but Nepal too was a place of adventures, scary moments, and swindlers. I found myself in frighteningly strange and potentially dangerous situations.

We spent hours on the train and buses before arriving at the border town. We arrived at 2 a.m. and the immigration office was not open until 4 a.m. The bus driver was kind enough to let us sleep on the bus, but rickshaw drivers were already waiting to transport us to our destination. At 4 a.m., the rickshaw drivers woke us up abruptly to take us to the immigration office. We followed them half-asleep to a place that appeared to be a dilapidated warehouse. It had been raining all night and the electricity was out. In the dark with the rain drizzling down, we were brought to this dilapidated building. It did not look legitimate and the possibility of being robbed and murdered seemed frightfully real.

We paid the rickshaw drivers to leave us. By 4:30 a.m., the office was still closed. One of my traveling companions called out, "Immigration!" and someone answered back, "Immigration opens at six o'clock!" We had no choice but to sit in the darkness, in a dilapidated warehouse and wait. At 5:30, the immigration officer came down and stamped our passports. We crossed over to Nepal and bought tickets from a man who claimed that it was a ticket to ride on his private bus. In actuality, it was a ticket for a government bus with many stops and we were charged twice as much.

Upon our arrival in Katmandu, I saw the difference between the capital of Nepal and the capital of India; Nepal was less crowded. It also seemed a lot cleaner. After a few relaxing days, we left for Pokhara, arriving four hours late because of a landslide.

My traveling companions and I had planned to do a trek in Pokhara, the legendary trek in Nepal, but after a day of hiking along the hillside, I accepted my physical limitations and withdrew from the plan. My traveling companions continued on their trek and I traveled alone. I met with other classmates and traveled to Chitwan National Park. After a few days, they also continued on with their journey and I was alone again.

As I wandered alone in Chitwan, I decided to participate in a jungle walk. Quite frankly, I did not want to encounter any animals while on foot. For the walk, I was supposed to get two guides; one walking in the front and one in the back, but one of them did not show up. I ventured into the jungle of Nepal with a guide whose only safety tip was to climb a tree if I see a rhino. How do I climb a tree in hiking boots? Ten minutes into the walk, I saw a bear. I tapped my guide on the back and pointed it out to him. We backed up slowly away from the bear but it saw us. I panicked and started running for my life, thinking that it might be my last few moments on Earth. My guide stopped running, screamed and pounded his stick on the ground to scare the bear. The bear got scared and ran away. I refused to return to the jungle and we walked along the river instead.

One story I like to tell about Nepal involved an encounter with a Nepali woman wearing a colorful sarong with a baby on her back. She asked if we wanted to rent a boat. We said no and she asked if we wanted some food.

We declined again and she asked if we wanted some refreshment, to which we also said no. Finally, she got to the point and asked if we wanted "magic mushroom."

Thailand: January 2000

In January of 2000, I met up with two of my friends from the study abroad program in Chiang Mai who had continued their stay after the program ended.

I visited Bangkok, although I had heard that Bangkok was just another big, polluted and crowded city. I found Bangkok to be clean and orderly after my experience in India. I was naïve when I thought Chiang Mai was dirty and chaotic. Nowadays, I know how much dirtier the world can be.

I left Chiang Mai and spent a few days in Krabie, a beautiful beach in Southern Thailand and then went back to Bangkok. I enjoyed the trip, walking around and buying all the sour fruits and salads—mangos, papayas, and *katot*. I also enjoyed the hospitality of a Thai friend who was married to a Cambodian-American man.

I was having lunch alone at a café when I noticed a lady that I presumed to be Thai sitting with her daughter. I could tell that her daughter was partly Caucasian. I struck up a conversation with her and it turned out that she was married to an American and for awhile she had also been living in India. At the time of our meeting, she and her daughter were living in San Francisco. She told me that her father is Cambodian and he was from Pailin, a province in Cambodia, and her daughter is named Pailin after her father's hometown.

Peru: June 2001

I saw a picture of Machu Picchu hanging on the wall of an acquaintance's home and I was inspired to visit. Peru somewhat reminded me of India. From the airport, we passed rundown, crowded buildings, trash scattered on the ground in every direction, half-torn posters plastered on billboards, buildings, walls, and poles, vendors selling food in their carts along the road, vendors standing in the middle of the highway in mad traffic trying to make a few cents. The driving was aggressive; the smell of smog and pollution burned my nose and a car rammed into us from behind. My driver and the other driver stopped to negotiate and the other person gave my driver some money for the damage.

That was my first impression of Peru and that was the extent of its similarity to India. Peru has its own charm and personality. It was very clean overall. Unlike most Asian countries, public affection between men and women is allowed. I saw couples kissing at the "Park of Love," and other designated places. I found the people of Peru to be charming, fun, and easy to handle. Most people would immediately leave you alone when you told them you didn't want something. They do not follow you, if you do not acknowledge them.

Machu Picchu was breathtaking, but for a moment I was disappointed. Machu Picchu really *was* a ruin. I was used to the temples of India and Cambodia, with their delicate sculptures and recognizable foundations, but I realized that the beauty of Machu Picchu is in the mountains surrounding it. No matter what direction you turn, the mountains were stunning, nature at her best.

In Ica, we stayed in a hotel near an Oasis, surrounded by sand dunes. I woke up early to hike the dunes.

We visited Hacienda San Jose, listening to stories of

the olden days of slavery and I heard the voices of their suffering. I was afraid to sleep alone in my hotel room after learning about the slave chambers and the tortures inflicted there.

In Peru, I did not have a "Cambodian encounter." But I met a Thai lady at the airport who was excited to see me. She came over and spoke Thai to me. I shook my head and told her that I did not understand. She then spoke Spanish but I shrugged again because I did not speak Spanish either despite taking four years of high school Spanish.

Mexico: December 2002 to January 2003

From December 25, 2002 to January 8, 2003, I traveled to Mexico to further my perspectives of the world. I went to Mexico to learn about the Zapatistas and their struggles. There were eighty people in the caravan, half from the U.S. and half from Mexico.

During the trip, everything that could have gone wrong did go wrong. And everything that was perfect and beautiful was perfect and beautiful.

The day after our arrival in Mexico City, we headed to Chiapas. The trip to Chiapas is approximately twenty-four-hours long but it took us over thirty hours. On the way there, we got into an accident. No one on our bus was hurt but there was a casualty in the other car. I was amazed at people's compassionate responses to the accident. Everyone did everything in their power to help, cutting the car door open to get the driver out, sitting with the children, comforting them and protecting them from the rain. The drivers of two nearby trucks transported the injured passengers to the hospital before the police and the ambulance arrived on the scene two hours later.

We continued with our trip and were eventually transferred to three community trucks, which took us to our temporary homes via unpaved back road that was four-hours long. We were squeezed inside the trucks with our belongings. There was no room to sit so we stood. I was so exhausted that I squeezed myself into a corner and fell asleep, standing up, leaning against a pile of backpacks. One truck broke down and the other had a flat tire. By the time we arrived in Chiapas, we had been traveling for thirty hours.

Our presence in Chiapas discouraged the government from using violence against the community and violating their human rights because an international community was present.

From December 29 to January 2, about forty-five hundred people arrived to celebrate the anniversary of the Zapatista revolution. We danced and celebrated with them every night.

We left Chiapas at 5 a.m. on January 3 and arrived in Mexico City at 4 a.m., January 4. We were scheduled to return January 2 but the thing that could have gone wrong did go wrong; there was no truck available to take us to the airport and quite a few people missed their flights. The rest of my time in Mexico was spent in Mexico City and nearby sites.

Costa Rica: August 2005

In August 2005, I spent a week in Costa Rica enjoying a beautiful country and a relaxing vacation. I visited national parks, a volcano, a pristine cloud forest, a beautiful waterfall, and several beaches. Costa Rica is a country that takes pride in being peaceful, and in not being poor, illiterate, or besieged by political turmoil. Costa Rica is proud of prospering without an army for over fifty years, confirming the general sentiment that they are a sanctuary of tranquility within a violent world. This is something that every country around the world should be proud to achieve and should try to achieve.

I saw Cambodia in the landscape of Costa Rica and I also stayed in a lodge that reminded me of a Cambodian hut surrounded by beautiful palm trees. Maybe someday, Cambodia can also take pride in being a country without war.

The world is a beautiful place. I have traveled far and wide and can vouch for it. The world is also an ugly place with ruthless and unforgiving acts that linger in the air and the memory of those who have suffered.

PART SIX

Remembrance and Celebration

New Year's Celebration

I have celebrated Khmer New Year with the Cambodian community of Long Beach since 1990 at El Dorado Park and Santa Fe Dam. New Year at the park is for celebrating with friends that we see every day as well as old friends that we have somehow lost touch with through the years. The celebration exemplifies the enjoyment of life and the gathering of people with the same history and background.

In Cambodia, the celebration of new year is a week-long event, but the most important dates are April 13th, 14th, and 15th when a new *Tevada* comes to earth and takes her post as the new guardian. New Year at my house is like spring-cleaning. My mother is adamant about cleaning the house and making it presentable for the new guardian. But it is also like Christmas as my mother decorates her shrine with lights, incenses, candles, and flowers. I see New Year as a combination of many holidays wrapped into one, a celebration of life and tradition, new and old.

Symbolically Significant

April 17, the day the Khmer Rouge declared victory, is a day of reckoning for Cambodia, but it has no real significance in my life. It has passed by like any other day, as it did even in 1975. Battambang had been captured, and I was eight days old. But thirty years later, in 2005, halfway around the world in Long Beach, California, the significance of April 17 led to an incident that divided the

community, exposing painful memories for many Cambodians.

The Cambodian community received the city's support to host a New Year parade in April 2005. In an unfor-
tunate coincidence, the date chosen to celebrate the parade
was Sunday, April 17. The date was chosen to follow the
celebration at El Dorado Park. Weeks prior to April 17,
the community met to plan the parade. An organization
called the Killing Field Memorial Task Force sprang up
to protest the insensitivity of the selected date.

Out of curiosity, I attended a meeting. I observed the
protests, listened, and argued with the protesters. Emotions were intense on both sides, the side who was against
the chosen date and the side who did not see an issue with
the date. The confrontation was shocking and frightening. I saw into the past and the emotional games that the
Khmer Rouge had played on a nation of people. I observed
the emotional games that were now played within the
Long Beach Cambodian community; the brainwashing
and the danger that came with it. I saw the insensitivity and the division that was unclear to most people, forc-
ing the corpse of the Khmer Rouge to rear its ugly head
in our emotionally beleaguered community. The division
seemed deep and there was little room for compromise. I
attended the city council meeting on Tuesday, April 5th,
and listened to protesters on both sides argue their case. I
was moved by some but annoyed with those who engaged
in theatrical productions. The city listened and agreed to
discuss a date change at the meeting on Thursday, April
7, 2005.

I was glad for the proposed date change, but I did not
have a problem with a parade on April 17. All through my
life, April 17 has not been a consciously significant day. I
could have been in class, at work, celebrating New Year
at the park, or attending the many parties in and around

Long Beach. I might have been at a temple, if it was a Sunday. Our New Year's celebration in Long Beach took place on the weekend closest to April 13–15, but New Year's parties occurred the weekend before and the weekend after.

I had never objected to celebrating and participating in any of the activities that took place in Long Beach for New Year so I had no objection to the parade. I even thought it would be symbolic of our survival and a celebration of life if the parade took place on that date. I have never heard of a memorial service held in Long Beach on April 17 to remember the victims of the Killing Fields. Nor was I surprised there had never been a memorial service, since most Cambodians do not celebrate anniversaries or birthdays either. I think most people remember the departed souls of their loved ones during *pchum ben*, the religious ceremony to honor and remember our ancestors.

But April 17 is a controversial and symbolic day no matter how you look at it. As a symbol, people may see what they want to see and feel what they want to feel. Just as Columbus is a controversial symbol—an explorer who discovered America, or a murdering thief?—April 17 can be a day to celebrate, or a day to mourn. No one can be forced to celebrate and no one should be forced to mourn.

The people who objected to a parade on April 17 viewed it as a symbolic day of mourning. I looked at a celebration on April 17 as symbolic of the Cambodian people's survival. The parade had a memorial component to it, which I thought was a fitting display of Cambodian culture and history as it includes the things we loved and celebrated and the things we are ashamed of, by remembering those we lost.

During the meeting on March 31, 2005, those who opposed holding a parade on April 17 protested with a candle vigil. After the meeting, I went outside to meet the pro-

testers and propose the idea of having an all-day memorial
service at the same time as the parade as an alternative
for those who could not with a clear conscience celebrate
on that day. But they did not agree to it. They did not
want a parade on that day, period. What followed was a
heated discussion, inflamed by innuendos and onlookers
commenting from the sidelines. They implied that I do not
know my own history and that I was the daughter of a
Khmer Rouge trying to furtively celebrate my heritage. I
tried to listen to the opposition and they tried to listen to
me, and we ended the discussion with a handshake and no
room for compromise.

I could not rule out April 17 as a day of celebration
because the Khmer Rouge took over different parts of
Cambodia on different day. I asked if we should avoid celebrating on April 9 because it was the day that Battambang
fell. I also pointed out that on most days in April, some
province, some people were affected. Should we not celebrate at all in April? There were also parts of Cambodia
that were taken over years before 1975. The significance
of April 17 paled in comparison to the sufferings inflicted
by the Khmer Rouge.

Many people professed that they mourned on April 17
of last year and previous years. I have my doubts. I was
told by an older gentleman *"to be Cambodian, one should
not celebrate on April 17."* I held my tongue out of respect. I
have never mourned on April 17 or any particular day for
what happened in Cambodia, but I have spent a great deal
of my life conflicted over the nature of humankind and our
cruelty. I do not have memories or traumatizing experiences but I have listened to stories, read different autobiographies, and watched documentaries that have affected
me deeply on an emotional and spiritual level. I have spent
a great deal of my life blaming God for atrocities around
the world. I may not be protesting the parade on April

17 but I have done my fair share of protesting, of being ashamed, and of mourning. For me, *To be Cambodian, you will eventually have to face the consequences of what our people did to each other, but I do not think that April 17 is necessarily the date on which that has to happen.* I came to terms with the history of Cambodia in my own way. Others may have different ways of dealing with it. I hope that all Cambodians will take the time to learn about the Killing Fields and come to terms with what happened, but no one should be forced to do so until they are ready.

The Final Confrontation

I drove to the meeting on April 7, 2005, with apprehension. I was relieved that the date had been changed but I did not know what to expect. As I approached McArthur Park, I saw protesters on the sidewalk holding signs and candles. The meeting was scheduled for 6:30 p.m. and Councilwoman Laura Richardson was attending to announce the date change. The conflict had reached its zenith and I was not in the mood to face more accusatory stares. I went through the backdoor after I parked my car.

Once inside, I stood next to students from California State University, Long Beach (CSULB), and felt safe enough to observe the crowd. We stared at each other, knowing that we were on different sides. I saw rage and anger in their faces and I knew they saw us as traitors. I felt disbelief at the atmosphere of rage and it increased as protesters began to scream at the college students, calling them the sons and daughters of the Khmer Rouge, telling them that by standing inside, they were ignorant of their own history and disrespecting their elders. I walked away as the insults escalated. Eventually, the students also disbursed, refusing to engage in verbal abuse and name-calling.

At 6:30 p.m., the people inside scrambled to find a seat, but the protesters would not join us. A protester came inside to request that the room be divided into two sides, separated by a space. A few protesters came inside, but the majority still refused to join the meeting. They screamed for a change of date. I had heard the date had been changed and that the meeting was merely a formality to announce it. Feeling rebellious about the seat division, I sat down on the protesters' side. Some protesters were strangers and some were people that I had known for years. I talked to them about trying to get people to come inside. We made signs and held them against the windows, but this gesture was ignored. People were screaming and running amok. I talked to an older woman, explaining that the date has been changed and beseeched her to ask people to come inside. She replied, "I know, daughter, but for some reasons they refused to come inside." For the first time since the conflict began, I experienced what it felt like to be addressed by a stranger with a term of endearment, in the very beautiful way that Cambodians address each other. I called her "aunty" and she called me "daughter." We were no longer fighting but remembering that we were family.

Councilwoman Richardson refused to start the meeting unless everyone came inside. She wanted the opportunity to reproach the protesters for their behavior. She stood her ground against the anger, and at the end of the meeting, I had a great deal of respect for her.

Amidst the chaos outside, someone yelled that to go inside means you agree to have the parade on April 17. It was a blatant lie used to rile the crowds. By then, I decided that my fear was unreasonable, that the people standing outside, screaming, running amok, were Khmer people and they would not harm me, no matter how angry they felt.

Someone screamed for a written memorandum as proof that the date had been changed.

I walked into the mist of angry protesters. I was ignored. Clueless Cambodians passing by asked for an update of what was going on and the protesters explained with exaggerated lies. The onlookers were told the protest was against a parade that celebrates the Khmer Rouge victory. I listened in disbelief but I proceeded with my plan. I infiltrated different groups telling them that the date has been changed and they should go inside to listen to the announcement. Some responded tersely that they have no reason to go inside. They wanted to see it written on paper so they could go home. Others said they could not go in because the "leaders" forbade them. Some were kind and said, they would go inside, and some politely refused. Another student was also outside trying to convince different people. Our eyes met, and we nodded at each other encouragingly.

I broke down when I was confronted by a woman who kept screaming about her brother who was killed by the Khmer Rouge. When I asked her to go inside, she screamed about all the family that she lost, her parents and her brother, about their death and that the Khmer Rouge had killed everyone in her family. She cried. My chest constricted and I too cried. I touched her arm and told her that the date was changed. After she calmed down, she walked away and eventually, she also went inside.

Slowly, more people went inside, but the chaos outside continued. The leaders themselves no longer agreed on the course of action. The crowd swarmed around the leaders listening for direction. A man stood up to tell the crowd they could not trust the councilwoman, pointing out that she had said the date would be changed to April 16, but now it was going to be changed to April 23; he pointed out the inconsistency and urged people not to go inside. I could not fathom his reasons for the division he was creating. Another man stood up, telling people that it would be beneficial to their cause to go inside. Finally, I heard a voice of reason and I wondered who he was. By then, there were enough people inside that the councilwoman was willing to start the meeting. I went inside, giving up on the stubborn few. From reading the *Press Telegram* the following day, I found out that the voice of reason was Chandara Hac.

The meeting was sobering, but there were joyous claps at the announcement of the date change. At the end, we hugged whether we meant it or not. I hugged a protester to shut her up. I also hugged people out of genuine relief.

The division also penetrated the bonds among friends and family. A father who protested a parade on April 17 may have had a son who did not see anything wrong with a parade on that date. The protest was against the insensitivity of rejoicing on the thirtieth anniversary of the Khmer Rouge victory, but the intensity of the unrest was in part based on lies and rumors that we were celebrating the anniversary of the Khmer Rouge victory. If people could get this angry at perceived insensitivity, imagine how much angrier and heartless they could be if they were recruited by the Khmer Rouge to fight real injustice—the exploitation of the poor peasants who made up the majority of the population. What cruelty might follow their battle against corrupted oppressors? Enough to cause two million deaths?

The Price of Victory

The date of the parade was changed so April 17 was available for mourning. Prior to April 17, I was engaged in planning a memorial service with CSULB students and friends who had held opposing views throughout the or-deal. We had been locked in heated debate, although we had tried to understand each other. With the date change, we reconciled by collaborating on a memorial service.

We learned that the Killing Field Memorial Task Force was already planning an event, so we offered our assistance. Upon meeting with a task force member, I was greeted with an apology. For this man, who was an elder in the community, to apologize was incredible. He apologized for any offenses, insults, and name-calling that may have happened. I graciously accepted his apology. I offered to create a brochure for the event. I included some of my writings and my beliefs that the remembrance should expand beyond the victims of the Killing Fields. We should remember the victims of the American bombings, the victims of the Cambodian civil war, and the Killing Fields.

I passed out hundreds of flyers during the celebration at El Dorado Park. I attended the service along with other CSULB students who were called sons and daughters of the Khmer Rouge. There were about fifty people at the event, a small fraction of those who had protested. But those who came were there to support the intention behind the event. We listened to the speeches, feeling whatever arose in remembrance of this tragic history. I have met people from the East Coast and the West Coast who want to establish a national recognition of April 17 as a day of remembrance for the victims of the Cambodian war and the Killing Fields. I support the idea of learning and remembering our past. For some, a day to specifically remember and mourn is needed, but others find their own ways to learn and come to terms with the past. For those who feel strongly enough to work toward establishing a national day of remembrance, I applaud you. You have your cause and I have mine. In the end, this should benefit all of us.

April 2005 was a true legacy of the Khmer Rouge. Our community experienced division, insults, threats, and broken windows. There was insensitivity on both sides; insensitivity regarding the chosen date and the length of time it took to change it, and insensitivity generated by insults and lies.

The Parade

On the morning of April 24, 2005, I woke up feeling elation and trepidation. I was excited about the parade, but I was coerced into marching in the parade in a colorful skimpy outfit as an indigenous Cambodian. I knew about the outfits, but I did not know that I had to coordinate it with dancing. Amidst the last-minute planning, commotion, and excitement, I had reservations about the parade and my role in it.

In the dressing room, I reluctantly took my costumes. A young high school girl asked me if I was in the indigenous group. I replied with an unenthusiastic affirmative. She offered to take my place since her sister and friends were also in it. I quickly handed her the clothes, delighted to be free of my duty. The president of the Cambodian Student Society (CSS) at CSULB, Lina Heng, saw the exchange. She invited me to walk in the parade with the student group and gave me Cham clothes, the costume of Cambodian Muslims, to wear. I went from being an indigenous person to a Muslim.

To begin, we lined up in the middle of Anaheim, on the corner of Junipero to hear the blessing offered by the monks and any last-minute instructions before marching down the street. CSS was the second group in the parade, behind the entourage of monks and elders in the community.

The energy, the sea of faces, and the community support for the parade were incredible. A huge crowd lined the street, clapping to the rhythm of the festivity. Along the way, I stared into the crowd, spotting the familiar faces of high school and college friends, of neighbors and people I had seen around the community. I knew it was going to be a great event. The college students wore a variety of Cambodian clothes representing different lifestyles and ethnic group. Some of the boys wore sarongs with sneakers. I gave them points for their effort although they did not realize that men wear a special type of sarong, not the same type that women wear.

Within our group, we had Chayam. They were the excitement of the parade, chanting, screaming, singing, and getting the crowd to clap and dance. Some spectators were so moved by the Chayam that they joined the parade and danced with us before taking their posts as spectators again.

The community was united in more ways than one by the parade. Beside the size of the crowd, the people who had protested against the parade were now marching in it and even sitting atop a float representing the guardian angels of the New Year.

Later, I saw pictures of the parade. The parade participants and the groups represented were diverse. Some of the floats were beautiful while other seemed strange and out of place and none of us were able to figure out what they represented.

I look forward to the parade of every coming year; I want to see and feel the festivities of New Year and to find a way to celebrate life and each other and to welcome the Angels who are sent to look after us.

PART SEVEN

Final Thoughts

Random

If I were born into a rich family in Cambodia, how willing would I be to share the wealth? I try to imagine myself in a position of power with people to wait on me, getting what I want, when I want—would I give it up? For a long, silent moment, the answer was scary.

• • •

The next voyage is through the stars. If we could, I would. For now, I am content with traveling the world. I love *Star Trek* and the world in which they live. The world of Captain Picard, Commander Ryker, and Deana Troy, is without war, poverty, or hunger. No one worries about encroachment or exploitation. The world of *Star Trek* is peaceful. Excitement for the storylines is attained through wars with peoples from other planets, while everyone on planet Earth coexists peacefully. Can we achieve this idealistic world? Do you want to live in that world? Some day, maybe the world and Cambodia will live the world of the Star Trekkers.

• • •

My love and devotion to sarongs is not a universal sentiment among Cambodians. Some view it as an inferior piece of clothing, drawing a distinction between upper class and lower class, poor versus rich, a city person versus a peasant from the countryside. I was asked in an accusing tone, "Why were you wearing sarong everywhere you go?" because there were many pictures of me in sarongs during my third trip to Cambodia. I feel feminine, soft, and beautiful in one, not to mention the practicality that comes with a sarong. It is easier to urinate behind a bush or a tree in a sarong than in jeans, I thought, but I was too tired to explain.

• • •

Survivor's guilt and accusations are plentiful. *You have no family members that died in the Killing Fields at all?* No. *You left Cambodia in 1975, escaping the atrocities that we suffered?* Yes. We are back to the same argument. Only *farmers* could escape being persecuted by the Khmer Rouge, so they are blamed for being in league with the Khmer Rouge. But the *connected high-ranking officials* of Cambodia were able to obtain asylum in other countries and escaped the Killing Fields all together. They too are blamed for being selfish cowards. Instead of inducing guilt in those who escaped in 1975 and those who did not lose family members in the Killing Fields, can you be glad that your countrymen were saved?

An Undisputed Truth

In Cambodia, my parents were farmers and their life was filled with the joy and tribulation of farming the land, celebrating the seasons, and praying to their ancestors. In Cambodia, the infrastructure for schools was limited, but both of my parents are literate. They have always reiterated the value of education. Just as middle-class American parents read fairy tales to their children, I grew up listening to the oral folktales and myths of Cambodia. My mother sang and recited Khmer poetry to me while my father told captivating stories. In exchange for these stories, I would do extra chores, which could have included plucking my father's beard or my mother's eyebrows.

There is a fallacious belief that Cambodians from the countryside do not value education. Education is a luxury in the life of farmers, but people encourage their children to obtain it whenever possible. They even choose the "smartest" kid and send him to school. Most male children are sent to temple to be shaped into literate people with a socially dictated morality.

Despite my parents' emphasis on education, my siblings and I do not perceive education in the same way. Research has shown the importance of encouraging young children to read and develop their imagination. This was the problem in my family and this is also the problem with many Cambodian parents who live in the ghettos and try to make ends meet—finding the time to read to their children, to tell them bedtime stories, and talk about Cambodia.

I grew up with fairy tales and folktales that nurtured my interest in reading and stimulated my imagination. My parents devised ways to help me learn English. One day, they taught me all the words that end with 'at' and all the letters in the alphabet that can be made into a word with 'at'. The next day, it would be the words ending in 'it'. Eventually, I outgrew their learning technique but I had been given a method to learn. I nurtured my own learning with different books, ranging from Dr. Seuss to Winnie-the-Pooh. By the time I was in high school, I spent hours reading, especially since I was not allowed to go out. My mother bragged about my studious nature and the many hours I spent locked in my room studying when in reality I was reading historical romances.

My siblings did not get to hear the fairy tales or the songs my mother sang. By the time they were growing up, the time allocated to making a living had become a priority. My family, like most Cambodian families, was on welfare. The welfare check was insufficient and many families lived together, cramped in small apartments. After three more children, the check from the Welfare Department became even less sufficient. There was a need to make money and to do more than make ends meet. There was a need to clothe and feed the children and obtain a few luxury items such as furniture. We also aimed to rent our own apartment even if it was just a one bedroom, to own a decent car, and to take an occasional vacation, (granted most of these "vacations" tended to be trips to Las Vegas). My parents were working twelve hours a day and they had no time to tell bedtime stories. There were still playtimes, but my three younger siblings did not get to experience the full affect of our parents' magical storytelling.

When faced with giving their children story time or working long hours to feed and clothe them, the choice was easy—you feed and clothe them first. My parents did not know this and neither did I, but in looking back, I have no doubt that the stories they shared with me promoted my interest in learning. I spent my time in primary and secondary school working toward entrance into a four-year institution of higher education, but this does not seem to be an important priority for all of my siblings.

The problem is the ensnaring cycle of poverty in which parents are taken away from their children.

In my mind's eye, I can divide the Cambodian community of Long Beach into two types based on their previous status in Cambodia, the rich city people and the poor farmers. The former has little problem making it in America. The latter group had to adjust to everything, the novelty of a kitchen sink and the luxury of a flushing toilet. I am familiar with the farmers of Cambodia, which include my parents, my neighbors, my parents' friends, and their children.

We are the children of farmers and parents who were

not educated with university degrees. Our parents broke the laws, used the system, and were paid under the table to make ends meet. Our parents were seasonal farm workers, picking strawberries and jalapenos. Our parents were sweatshop workers, sewing clothes in their own homes, in the garage, or at the factories twelve hours a day and getting paid anywhere from thirty cents to a dollar-something for each outfit they assembled. These jobs do not offer medical coverage so many Cambodians opt for welfare. With welfare, our parents receive Medicare. If they were to give up welfare and officially work full-time on menial jobs, there is no guarantee that they would be able to afford health benefits for themselves or for us.

I have seen the sweat and toil that many Cambodians endure to make a living in America and provide their children with the necessities of life along with some minor luxuries. Our parents encouraged us to pursue higher education, but people need to understand the importance of engaging us at an early age.

In America, my parents have been welfare recipients, industrious workers, laborers, law breakers, bakers and cashiers at a donut shop, tax-paying citizens and sweat-factory workers, sewing clothes in a cramped, dusty garage. But mostly, they have been loving parents who worked long hours to give their children a decent life and a better future. They want us to have a white-collar job and a life of relative wealth. In particular, they want us to be endowed with education and the ability to know right from wrong and be decent human beings. This is an undisputed truth that I know.

Do You Speak Khmer or Cambodian?

Person A: *Do you speak Khmer or Cambodian?*

Person B: *Does it matter? I speak the language no matter what you call it.*

Person A: *Anyway, I thought* Cambodian *is the people from Cambodia and* Khmer *is the language spoken by the people from Cambodia.*

Person B: *I thought* Khmer *and* Cambodian *mean the people and the language.*

Person A: *My high school Spanish teacher was a Caucasian woman. She called me over to her desk and asked me, "What language do you speak at home?" I told her, "Cambodian." She responded sharply, "No, you do not speak Cambodian.* Cambodian *is the people and the language is* Khmer. *You speak* Khmer, *not Cambodian."*

Person B: *I think she is wrong.*

Person A: *I have asked different people on this and the answer is about fifty-fifty.*

Person B: *Someone is wrong…*

Person A: *On that day, I was embarrassed to be reprimanded by a white woman for not understanding words used to describe my language, but I have never repeated that mistake again. I speak Khmer. But I have seen it in writing, even with the academic community, giving* Cambodian *as a language option.*

Person B: *The academic community is bigger than your high school teacher.*

Person A: *Do you want to join my crusade?*

Person B: *A crusade for what?*

Person A: *To cross out the word* Cambodian *and write in* Khmer.

Person B: *What for?*

Person A: *For the word* Khmer *to be associated with* Cambodia. *If the world can associate* Tagalog *as a language spoken by the people of the Philippines, how hard it is to get people to associate* Khmer *as the language spoken by the people of Srok Khmer?*

Person A: *For you, I will speak only Khmer.*

Navy

Two syllables. Simple and easy. It is pronounced with a short "a." Nā-vee. Many people chose an American name in place of their Khmer name. I wanted to keep mine, even though 99 percent of the time, people who see it for the first time mispronounce it. They would say, "'Nā-vee,' interesting name." Once I corrected them, most people would say, "That's pretty."

I do not think less of people who change their names or allow others to say their name incorrectly. There are many Khmer names that non-Khmer will not be able to say correctly. There are plenty of non-Khmer names that I will never be able to say correctly. The few people who have gotten my name correct on their own are bilingual Spanish and English speakers because the 'a' sound is also short in their language.

In my first job after college, a lady called me and said, "Navy, this is so-and-so from so-and-so, and I need the information for so-and-so." As I was trying to search for the information she needed, she said, "Navy, don't you want to know how I was able to pronounce your name correctly?" I hadn't noticed but she did pronounce it correctly during our first encounter. I said, yes, pleasantly surprised. She said, "Well, my son is dating a Khmer girl and her name is also Navy. She taught me how to pronounce it the right way."

Features of Beauty

The beauty of Earth is embedded in its landscapes and the features of its people. In my travels, I have seen beauty in the untamed wilderness and unparalleled peace in the morning dew and crashing waves along endless stretches of colorful sand. I have seen sands of different colors and peoples of different customs, dressed in a variety of ways, beautifying Earth beyond my dreams and imagining.

Beauty is written across the features of Earth and the faces of all peoples, features that are unique from country to country and similar across the world.

Most Cambodians and other Asians see beauty in skin color and the shape of the eyes. Many facial products in Cambodia include an ingredient that lightens the skin. I have seen news reports about young girls in Asian countries who undergo surgery to remove the epicanthic fold over their eyelids.

Beauty comes in a can and out of a surgeon's office. These beauty features have created a complex for many people in a world that subscribes to a fixed set of beauty standards that our genes do not always permit. I have discovered self-acceptance, but as yet I still have a prescribed set of beauty standards, which include a sharp nose and big eyes with curly lashes. Within Cambodia, a sharp nose and big eyes with curly lashes are seen as the remnants of an Indian prince creating the look of *Koun Kloung*. They are Indian features. I do think that some of the most beautiful women in the world are Indian women, and Khmer women are some of the most beautiful in the world.

Despite my prescribed standards of beauty, I have seen beauty that extends beyond these criteria. Ultimately, beauty does not rest in individual features but rather in *how those features work together*. Beauty is also in your attitude and how you carry yourself.

I know a Cambodian woman with a noticeably flat nose, but her facial features complement each other, producing an aura of beauty that is tangible. But this beautiful woman has a complex about her nose and had surgery to get a high-ridged, sharp nose. Once she had a new nose, I no longer saw the aura that was part of her beauty. There was something about the way she looked; the way her facial features complemented each other, that made her beautiful in my eyes; and the highly prized sharp nose took it away.

I have heard and seen statements that allude to light skin as a sign of beauty among Cambodians within my family, circle of friends, and strangers. *She is beautiful but a little bit too dark*. What a strange statement!

People rarely evaluate their own biases. For shock value, I have boldly stated that I think tight eyes without eyelids are ugly, because people with these eyes tend to be the same people who point out that dark skin is unattractive. I can quickly see the beauty in big round eyes; because they fit my ideal, but beauty can exist beyond this. I have known people who are beautiful whether they have sharp nose or flat nose, eyes with an epicanthic fold or without.

There is always something we lack or something we have and can admire about ourselves. If we could only accept what we have, we would feel so much better about ourselves. If we could only see beyond biases and preferences, the world would be so much more beautiful.

Linking the Past

The serene feature of Jayavaraman, the ancient God-King of Cambodia, is familiar among Cambodians. Sculptures of his face are an important part of many Cambodian artworks. His is also the face on the temple of Bayon, smiling peacefully upon his subjects, possessing the attributes of God, all-knowing and all-seeing, with his face looking out in all four directions. Many Cambodians have looked upon his face and compared their own features with his, seeing a resemblance and feeling pride in being the descendent of the God-King.

The full-lips of Khmer features come from the famous features of Jayavaraman. This is an attribute that is prevalent in my own family. We have noted that each family has a child that possesses the luscious fullness of the ancient Khmer's lips.

Between my parents, my mother has the fullest lips. My siblings and I inherited our parents' features, one or the other or a combination of both. My lips are a cross between the two of them. Some of our noses are sharp, taking after my mother, while others have a flare, taking after my father. Our noses, our lips, can they be those of Jayavaraman?

My mother and sister have the fullest, most beautiful Khmer lips. My sister has been asked on many occasions if she is Mexican. As a Cambodian, I feel as though I am related to the world, passing as a local in the towns and cities of many countries. A classmate once thought I had African roots because I was learning Swahili. He could not think of any reason for me to study Swahili unless I was African. I studied it because I want to visit Africa some day.

Family Resemblance

I look more like my aunts and cousins in Cambodia than I do my own sister and mother. I noticed the family resemblance and saw my mother's lips and eyes in my aunts and cousins. I saw myself in their faces.

I also saw exhaustion in their faces and demeanors

as they carried the burden of farming and laboring away on the land. I saw their hope for something better, but I cannot give it. At best, I have been a disappointment to many people who thought I was a savior. Many in Cambodia believe that their lot in life will improve because they have rich relatives in America, but I am far from being rich, and I only know how to survive from check to check, saving enough here and there to quench my passion for world travel. Most of my trips transpired through different study abroad programs when I was an undergraduate taking out loans to study and travel. Now, I save enough to take a trip here and there and go abroad at least once a year, but not enough to save anyone else without quenching my own thirst first. I cannot save them from poverty when I can barely save myself.

Our faces mirror so much more than our family resemblance. They highlight our hopes and disappointments. I see their disappointment, which has a way of reaching across distance and oceans.

I see the resemblance even in the little ones. My sister's daughter, Kayla, is a little girl with the most amazingly beautiful round eyes with thick, curly lashes. She smiles sweetly at the camera. Her eyes are wide and intense. When I juxtaposed a picture of Kayla's next to my cousin's son in Cambodia, I see that his eyes are as intense and just as passionate, but he is a Cambodian boy, born to farmers, and his life will be one of struggle. He stares at the camera without a smile as though he already knows that life as a farmer will be wearisome and tiring with its manual labor and hard work.

Voices of Remembrance

Reflecting on the atrocities in human history, I hear stories of suffering and voices of regret echoing through the walls, the history books, and time. My skin crawls, and I shiver in disbelief. I feel it in Toul Sleng. I feel it in the Museum of Tolerance, in the written words and the footage of the atrocities. I feel it in reading *Becoming Evil: How Ordinary People Commit Genocide and Mass Killing* by James Waller. I have listened and felt, but now I write a story of the atrocities around the world.

Voices of Regret: Cambodia's Killing Fields

I was an old lady of fifty-five when they took over our country. They were mean and disrespectful, wearing black, a color with no life. But my grief had begun long before they won the war. In 1973, they came into my village and took away my sixteen-year-old son. I have been a widow for ten years and he was all that I had. He did not want to go but they abducted him at gunpoint. They wanted him to fight with them against the Lon Nol Army saying it was his duty to free the people of Cambodia. Two years later, when they took over, I thought I would see my son again but I never did. For two years, I toiled away in the communal farmland. I have farmed all of my life but never with the schedule that the Khmer Rouge imposed on us. I slaved away and did not get enough to eat. I was tired. Too tired to move, I rested. *A little rest.* One of them came by and told me to get back to work. I beseeched him, "Nephew, I am so tired, please let me rest a little." He got angry and beat me with a hoe. That is how I died. I remembered hoping to myself that my son was dead. I hope that he has never beaten another human being to death with a hoe.

• • •

I lay awake tonight knowing it was the last night of my life. This is all the torture I could endure. I am ready to die. All I need to do is close my eyes. I want to savor this moment and the pain that courses through my body like tiny needles pricking inside out. My bones felt brittle. I gave them a confession. I am the enemy. I confess to it all, but my darling, I do not remember it. I only know it was a declaration of lies. Do I regret confessing a lie? Do I regret dying by the hands of my comrades? I have swallowed all of my regrets and I am taking them with me to my grave. I died fighting for the wrong side. But I died fighting for a worthy cause. I believe in the cause even now. I was young and impressionable. I joined the Khmer Rouge to free the people of Cambodia, but Death is setting me free. I feel the lightness in my bones, lifting away the pains and regrets. I close my eyes, seeking out the darkness. I close my eyes to remember your face. You and I joined the Khmer Rouge to fight for a cause, but the cause has been changed. We fought with them to free the oppressed but they have become the worst kind of oppressors. Wherever you are, my darling, I hope you do not feel what I feel. I am ready to die, taking with me a small victory, dying before they can torture again.

The Pedagogy of Misery

I read the *Pedagogy of the Oppressed* by Paulo Freire and saw the history of Cambodia in his words: "the oppressed become the oppressors." The Khmer Rouge began as a force to fight against oppression, only to oppress even more, fighting to end corruption and exploitation, only to destroy hearts and souls. Did the Khmer Rouge model the oppressors? In Cambodian society, the rich and powerful treated their subordinates as subhuman. The Khmer Rouge grew under this society whether they were the top leaders or the "poor, uneducated followers" who had been treated as subhuman all of their life. When they were in power, it was easy for them to do what their oppressors had been doing to them. They had lived and learned to view everyone under them as subhuman.

Freire also asserts that the oppressors view the oppressed as "ungrateful" and "envious," regarding them "as potential enemies who must be watched." I saw a thread on the Internet asking, "Who are the Khmer Rouge?" A seventeen-year-old girl answered, "My father told me that they were a bunch of ignorant and uneducated farmers who were jealous of the city people." Can she accept that her father is the ignorant prig who contributes to the rise and victory of the Khmer Rouge?

Year Zero

Year Zero—how do I describe the footage in the documentary or my feelings? It is heartbreaking but the word *heartbreak* cannot describe the anguish that pierces my soul. I saw women and children following their husbands and fathers into the war. I saw families being separated from each other as heartbreak and sadness engulfs their lives. I saw mutilated bodies after the rockets crashed into the city. This footage leaves me feeling empty and raw. I am mentally, physically, and emotionally desolate. I curl up into a ball searching for comfort by distorting my body into a less significant mass.

The images of dead bodies littering the countryside of Cambodia send terror through my body. My skin crawls, my breathing becomes shallow, and my heart is erratic, beating angrily and painfully. I hate the images of war and death. I hate the sorrow and the feeling of helplessness that overcomes me. I hate the cruelty of the Khmer Rouge. I hate feeling the anger and the hatred.

The film forces me to face my ignorance and my fears. It educates me about Cambodia and the horrors that my people have suffered. There is glimpse of hope in the motions of life, living and surviving war and its horrors, healing and smiling again. But Cambodia and her people are far from healed…

East Timor: The Incense Smoke

The incense smoke rises like a silent prayer for the people in a land far away as pain and fear grips the last moments of their lives. They seek refuge in a house of religion, but they are not saved. The incense smoke rises like a prayer for a land far away: East Timor, 1975 and 1991.

Rwanda: The Incestuous Slaughter

Like Cambodia, brother killed brother, Hutu and Tutsi, peasant versus bourgeoisie. Cruelty beyond words. Annihilation and destruction of your own soul at the confused hand of anger and hatred. Too shocking for words. Too stunning to move. I cry for you too. The face of the Killers has stained the progeny of the human race because every Killer is a human being or was a human being.

Mayan Butchers in a Guatemalan Village

The most vindictive and heartless killers are those who kill you with your own hands. They take away your children and indoctrinate them with hatred that eradicates their connection to their past and community.

The Mayan Butchers—you were abducted to become killers. You forget who you are and what you are capable of and where love truly dwells. Come home to wholeness. Find your way back to the Mayan heart. I hear their screams of pains, why can't you? I see the crease of grief in their faces, why can't you?

Srebrenica: Sound of Evil

Torture and laughter echo with the sounds of evil. To those who have died a violent death, may your heaven make up for what your fellow human beings on Earth refused to give to you—a beautiful life and a peaceful death.

This is a prayer for all human beings: may Heaven compensate for the misery on Earth. I am aware of many atrocities and feel so much more than I can express, but I hear other voices and feel other pains, so I remember. There is so much to learn and be wary of... the world needs to learn it too. Learn from it and each other to erase the violence and cruelty in our history and replace it with compassion and sensitivity... What a world it could be!

Echoes

We, the world, drone on and on about injustice and the exploitation of our land and people while we continue to exploit and inflict injustice. China complains about the Japanese occupation, but their occupation of Tibet slips their mind. Japan complains about the atomic bomb but tries to erase the rape of China from their history books. Vietnam thinks Cambodia is racist and unreasonable for fearing that Vietnam is trying to steal the heart of Cambodian souls, but Vietnam has forgotten that she too, is suspicious and fearful of being dominated and belittled by China.

Oh, Cambodia, your children are worried. Their land, country, and culture will suffocate under occupation, and they too, may die. Oh, Cambodian children, do not succumb to hatred. I know that it is easier said than done… But for some reason, I believe we will survive. I close my eyes and wait for the magic of our land to show us the way, to tell us the truth, and to protect us from evil, whether it is the evil inside or the evil outside. But if we should die, let us die with dignity. Let us die gracefully, forgiving those who trespass against us.

Kampuchea Krom

Kampuchea is another word for Khmer. *Kampuchea Krom* means *Khmer Below* (the southern part of Cambodia). The southern part of Cambodia has become a Lost World, a land that was given to a foreign country by another foreign country, and a new identity was forced upon her children. Kampuchea Krom was given to Vietnam on May 21, 1949, by the French (as if the French had any right to give her away). The people in Kampuchea Krom are called "Vietnamese of Khmer origin" by the Vietnamese government, but they consider themselves to be Khmer living in *Srok Khmer Krom*. Like the Mayan in Guatemala, they have suffered persecutions and massacres. They are still struggling to survive, struggling for their basic human rights.

I know little about Khmer history; I know even less about Kampuchea Krom and their plights. When I finally allowed myself to learn their history, it awakened the same feelings I had about the Killing Fields, the Holocaust, and so many other genocides. *Genocide*: the classification has become so meaningless. I feel their pain and suffering, but I can do nothing to help. I can only ignore it. Genocide is not even the past. It is still their present, still their suffering.

I have heard passing stories about my maternal grandmother who was originally from Kampuchea Krom. Grandmother spoke with a Kampuchea Krom accent but all of her children have a Battambang accent. It is strange to think that my mother and her mother spoke with two different voices.

There was a love story involved in my grandmother's journey into Battambang, but I cannot remember the details. My grandfather, who was from Battambang, went all the way to Kampuchea Krom to court my grandmother. During the courtship, my grandmother tested my grandfather by asking for help, and he was able to accomplish everything she wanted so she agreed to marry him and relocate to Battambang. My grandfather was a widower with children from a previous marriage, but my grandmother married him and became a mother to all his children. They also had their own children. My mother is their youngest child.

I finally understood the affinity that my mother felt for our Vietnamese-Cambodian neighbors who were originally from Kampuchea Krom. She must have heard her mother's voice in them.

My mother befriended them with the same kindness, friendliness, and charity that she employed with everybody, and they have been friends for the past twenty years. In a way, their friendship is a sad story. These family friends love my mother and like many Cambodians who become close friends, they want to validate their friendship by marrying into each other's family. They have tried and tried to no avail. They have tried to engage my aunt with their sons. When she refused to accept a marriage to one, they would bring the other and the other. But she continued to say no.

Enough with my digression, I should get back to Kampuchea Krom. It is a place of sadness, but they are a people of strength. They make us proud. They have united under a front to fight for their rights. I see no hope that they will gain autonomy, but as they themselves state on their website:

> Absolutely, they would like to have their own independent country and be responsible for their own future. However, one of their major objectives is "to develop peace, harmony, respect, understanding and cooperation between the Khmer Krom people and others, including the Vietnamese people." Therefore, the Khmer Krom people did not rule out other forms of self-determination.

www.khmerkrom.org

I, too, hope that they will know peace, harmony, respect, understanding, and cooperation. I hope they continue to be proud of being Khmer and persevere for the right and freedom to be Khmer. Khmer Krom is the Zapatista of Cambodia.

Ending the Excursion

I am not special and neither is Cambodia. Many souls have been born into wars. Many souls are lost; many more are broken, trying to make sense of their experiences and heal. There are many Cambodians… like Rwanda and others…hanging on for life. I reflect upon and remember them… I forget sometimes, and sometimes, I forget on purpose.

In each moment I remember, I send thoughts of compassion, an emotion each dying soul asked for, but did not receive.

I have struggled with dilemmas and I want to end this book with one that I am not sure I have resolved: Are pity and compassion the same emotion? Pity has a negative connotation. I feel compassion for the world, but do I have compassion for perpetrators of mass killing, or is it pity? Even if it is pity, should I not even have these feelings for perpetrators? I despise the perpetrators of crime against humanity, but strangely enough, I do feel compassionate toward the object of my hatred. I despised Pol Pot, and I have imagined the torture I would inflict if given the opportunity to punish him. But when I saw him in the mock trial, he was a frail, sickly shadow of a human being, old and dying. I felt sorry for him. He was merely a pitiful, frail-looking old man in need of compassion. I no longer want to punish him.

I felt sorry for Saddam Hussein when I saw the bewildered look on his face after his capture. It was too pitiful for me to continue hating him.

In watching the news about "children for sale," I hated the pimps and madams that sold them to pedophiles. I could have choked each pimp with my bare hands. But when they were captured, they looked pitiful and frightened; I felt a surge of pity for them then.

Since the war in Iraq started, I have felt compassion for American soldiers and their families and for the Iraqi soldiers and their families. Instead of thinking of our soldiers versus the enemy, I think of the families who worry about their children going off to war. I know that both sides are worrying about them equally. I can feel the human agony and worry spread across the world.

I write in hope and anger. I write to capture the laughter and share the hope...in honor of all human beings and our right to live and die with dignity, not in shallow graves.

About the Author

Navy Phim came to the United States in 1984 when she was nine years old. She graduated from the University of California, Los Angeles in 1999 with a Bachelor's Degree in English and Anthropology. She also received a Master of Science in Counseling, Student Development in Higher Education from California State University, Long Beach in December 2006. Navy is a world traveler and has returned to Thailand and Cambodia. She has also visited England, Scotland, India, Nepal, Peru, Mexico, Costa Rica and Canada.

To learn more about the author, the book and her future endeavors, visit: http://www.navyphim.com.